LifeChange

S E R I E S

A NavPress Bible study on the books of

1, 2 & 3 JOHN

NAVPRESS

A MINISTRY OF THE NAVIGATORS
P.O. BOX 35001, COLORADO SPRINGS, COLORADO 80935

The Navigators is an international Christian organization. Jesus Christ gave His followers the Great Commission to go and make disciples (Matthew 28:19). The aim of The Navigators is to help fulfill that commission by multiplying laborers for Christ in every nation.

NavPress is the publishing ministry of The Navigators. NavPress publications are tools to help Christians grow. Although publications alone cannot make disciples or change lives, they can help believers learn biblical discipleship, and apply what they learn to their lives and ministries.

Sixth printing, 1992

Printed in the United States of America

CONTENTS

ACKNOWLEDGMENTS

This LIFECHANGE study has been produced through the coordinated efforts of a team of Navigator Bible study developers and NavPress editorial staff, along with a nationwide network of fieldtesters.

SERIES EDITOR: KAREN HINCKLEY

HOW TO USE THIS STUDY

Objectives

Most guides in the LIFECHANGE series of Bible studies cover one book of the Bible. This one covers three books by the same author. Although the LIFECHANGE guides vary with the books they explore, they share some common goals:

    1. To provide you with a firm foundation of understanding and a thirst to return to the book;

    2. To teach you by example how to study a book of the Bible without structured guides;

    3. To give you all the historical background, word definitions, and explanatory notes you need, so that your only other reference is the Bible;

    4. To help you grasp the message of the book as a whole;

    5. To teach you how to let God's Word transform you into Christ's image.

    Each lesson in this study is designed to take 60 to 90 minutes to complete on your own. The guide is based on the assumption that you are completing one lesson per week, but if time is limited you can do half a lesson per week or whatever amount allows you to be thorough.

Flexibility

LIFECHANGE guides are flexible, allowing you to adjust the quantity and depth of your study to meet your individual needs. The guide offers many optional questions in addition to the regular numbered questions. The optional questions, which appear in the margins of the study pages, include the following:

    Optional Application. Nearly all application questions are optional; we hope you will do as many as you can without overcommitting yourself.

    For Thought and Discussion. Beginning Bible students should be able to handle these, but even advanced students need to think about them. These questions frequently deal with ethical issues and other biblical principles. They often offer cross-references to spark thought, but the references do not give obvious answers. They are good for group discussions.

For Further Study. These include: a) cross-references that shed light on a topic the book discusses, and b) questions that delve deeper into the passage. You can omit them to shorten a lesson without missing a major point of the passage.

If you are meeting in a group, decide together which optional questions to prepare for each lesson, and how much of the lesson you will cover at the next meeting. Normally, the group leader should make this decision, but you might let each member choose his or her own application questions.

As you grow in your walk with God, you will find the LIFECHANGE guide growing with you—a helpful reference on a topic, a continuing challenge for application, a source of questions for many levels of growth.

Overview and Details

The study begins with an overview of 1 John. The key to interpretation is context—what is the whole passage or book *about*?—and the key to context is purpose—what is the author's *aim* for the whole work? In lesson one you will lay the foundation for your study of 1 John by asking yourself, "Why did the author (and God) write the book? What did they want to accomplish? What is the book about?"

In lessons two through eleven you will analyze successive passages of 1 John in detail. Thinking about how a paragraph fits into the overall goal of the book will help you to see its purpose. Its purpose will help you see its meaning. Frequently reviewing a chart or outline of the book will enable you to make these connections.

In lesson twelve, you will review 1 John, returning to the big picture to see whether your view of it has changed after closer study. Review will also strengthen your grasp of major issues and give you an idea of how you have grown from your study.

Lessons thirteen and fourteen each cover one of John's shorter letters. Because of their brevity, they do not require separate overviews and reviews. They elaborate on certain themes raised in 1 John.

Kinds of Questions

Bible study on your own—without a structured guide—follows a progression. First you observe: What does the passage *say*? Then you interpret: What does the passage *mean*? Lastly you apply: How does this truth *affect* my life?

Some of the "how" and "why" questions will take some creative thinking, even prayer, to answer. Some are opinion questions without clearcut right answers; these will lend themselves to discussions and side studies.

Don't let your study become an exercise of knowledge alone. Treat the passage as God's Word, and stay in dialogue with Him as you study. Pray, "Lord, what do you want me to see here?" "Father, why is this true?" "Lord, how does this apply to my life?"

It is important that you write down your answers. The act of writing clarifies your thinking and helps you to remember.

Study Aids

A list of reference materials, including a few notes of explanation to help you make good use of them, begins on page 143. This guide is designed to include enough background to let you interpret with just your Bible and the guide. Still, if you want more information on a subject or want to study a book on your own, try the references listed.

Scripture Versions

Unless otherwise indicated, the Bible quotations in this guide are from the New International Version of the Bible. Other versions cited are the Revised Standard Version (RSV), the New American Standard Bible (NASB), and the King James Version (KJV).

Use any translation you like for study, preferably more than one. A paraphrase such as The Living Bible is not accurate enough for study, but it can be helpful for comparison or devotional reading.

Memorizing and Meditating

A psalmist wrote, "I have hidden your word in my heart that I might not sin against you" (Psalm 119:11). If you write down a verse or passage that challenges or encourages you, and reflect on it often for a week or more, you will find it beginning to affect your motives and actions. We forget quickly what we read once; we remember what we ponder.

When you find a significant verse or passage, you might copy it onto a card to keep with you. Set aside five minutes during each day just to think about what the passage might mean in your life. Recite it over to yourself, exploring its meaning. Then, return to your passage as often as you can during your day, for a brief review. You will soon find it coming to mind spontaneously.

For Group Study

A group of four to ten people allows the richest discussions, but you can adapt this guide for other sized groups. It will suit a wide range of group types, such as home Bible studies, growth groups, youth groups, and businessmen's studies. Both new and experienced Bible students, and new and mature Christians, will benefit from the guide. You can omit or leave for later years any questions you find too easy or too hard.

The guide is intended to lead a group through one lesson per week. However, feel free to split lessons if you want to discuss them more thoroughly. Or, omit some questions in a lesson if preparation or discussion time is limited. You can always return to this guide for personal study later. You will be able to discuss only a few questions at length, so choose some for discussion and others for background. Make time at each discussion for members to ask about anything they didn't understand.

Each lesson in the guide ends with a section called "For the group." These sections give advice on how to focus a discussion, how you might apply the lesson in your group, how you might shorten a lesson, and so on. The group leader should read each "For the group" at least a week ahead so that he or she can tell the group how to prepare for the next lesson.

Each member should prepare for a meeting by writing answers for all of the background and discussion questions to be covered. If the group decides not to take an hour per week for private preparation, then expect to take at least two meetings per lesson to work through the questions. Application will be very difficult, however, without private thought and prayer.

Two reasons for studying in a group are accountability and support. When each member commits in front of the rest to seek growth in an area of life, you can pray with one another, listen jointly for God's guidance, help one another to resist temptation, assure each other that the other's growth matters to you, use the group to practice spiritual principles, and so on. Pray about one another's commitments and needs at most meetings. Spend the first few minutes of each meeting sharing any results from applications prompted by previous lessons. Then discuss new applications toward the end of the meeting. Follow such sharing with prayer for these and other needs.

If you write down each other's applications and prayer requests, you are more likely to remember to pray for them during the week, ask about them at the next meeting, and notice answered prayers. You might want to get a notebook for prayer requests and discussion notes.

Notes taken during discussion will help you to remember, follow up on ideas, stay on the subject, and clarify a total view of an issue. But don't let note-taking keep you from participating. Some groups choose one member at each meeting to take notes. Then someone copies the notes and distributes them at the next meeting. Rotating these tasks can help include people. Some groups have someone take notes on a large pad of paper or erasable marker board (pre-formed shower wallboard works well), so that everyone can see what has been recorded.

Page 146 lists some good sources of counsel for leading group studies. The *Small Group Letter*, published by NavPress, is unique, offering insights from experienced leaders every other month.

INTRODUCTION

Map of the Roman Empire

The other apostles were dead, but John remained—the last living intimate friend of Jesus. The aged apostle was living in Ephesus, a port city Paul first evangelized four decades earlier. John regarded the Christians in every town within a hundred miles as his personal responsibility, and now a clique of pseudo-Christian teachers was wreaking confusion in John's flock. His response was a letter sent to each church in the province of Asia, the letter we call 1 John.

Timeline of John's Ministry

(All dates are approximate)

Jesus' public ministry	28-30 AD
John an apostle in Jerusalem	30-70
Jewish rebellion	66-70
Romans destroy Jerusalem, Christians flee	70
John in Ephesus	70-95
Domitian is Emperor of Rome	81-96
Gospel of John written	85-90
Epistles of John written	90-94
Domitian persecutes Christians; John is exiled to the island of Patmos and writes Revelation	95-96
John in Ephesus until his death	96-100

John

On page 9 is a likely reconstruction of what prompted the writing of 1 John.[1] John probably wrote this epistle around 90 AD, sixty years after Jesus' crucifixion and perhaps twenty-five after Paul's and Peter's deaths.

During Jesus' lifetime, John was one of the three disciples closest to Him (Luke 8:51, 9:28). When Jesus died, He entrusted His mother to John's care (John 19:26-27). In his Gospel, John called himself "the disciple whom Jesus loved" (13:23).

Popular mythology has sometimes painted John as a kindly old saint, like Santa Claus. Kind he may have been to his flock, but he had another face. Mark tells us that John and his brother James were known as the "Sons of Thunder" (Mark 3:17). They once offered to call down fire from heaven upon some Samaritans who snubbed Jesus (Luke 9:51-56). Jesus rebuked this zeal, but we can sense a sanctified Son of Thunder behind many passages of 1 John (1:6; 2:4,22; 3:9,18; 4:5-6,20; 5:10).

When Paul visited Jerusalem around 50 AD, John was still living there (Galatians 2:9). But in 70 AD the Roman armies demolished Jerusalem after crushing a Jewish revolt. The Christians fled. John went to Ephesus, where he became the thriving church's most venerable elder. By the time he wrote the fourth Gospel and his epistles, John was renowned throughout Asia, for he apparently traveled and preached frequently.[2]

10

In the 70s and 80s AD, persecution of Christians was a small-scale affair—a brawl here, a little job discrimination there, and malicious gossip nearly everywhere. But about 95 AD, Emperor Domitian took a dislike to Christianity, which many Romans considered a pernicious superstition. As one of its founders, John was exiled to the island of Patmos, where he beheld the visions recorded in the book of Revelation. When Domitian died in 96 AD, John returned to Ephesus and apparently died peacefully around 100 AD. He probably wrote his Gospel and epistles five or ten years before his Patmos sojourn.[3]

Syncretism

If persecution was only a minor irritant for the churches of Asia in 90 AD, heresy was a major threat. The Roman province of Asia, part of what is now called Asia Minor or Turkey (see the map on page 9), was a cultural melting pot. Greek conquerors had brought their language, philosophy, art, and religion from the west, while immigrants from Egypt, Persia, and Syria were carrying their customs from the east and mixing them with whatever ancient ways still lingered in Asia. Few people judged it necessary to hold one school of thought rigorously. There were many roads to truth, and a man took what he liked from each—a pinch of Plato, a dash of Persian dualism, and one's ancestral cult for tradition's sake. Modern scholars call this mixing of Greek and Oriental culture *syncretism*; it was pluralism taken to extremes.

In this environment, Jews and Christians were considered narrow-minded and impious for paying homage to just one God. Most people acknowledged hundreds and favored several deities. Some hedged their bets by joining one or more "mystery" cults—groups with secret rites of initiation that promised encounters with the divine and bliss in the afterlife. There were sects that mixed Judaism with Plato or astrology or secret revelation. Thus, it was inevitable that someone would try to add Christianity to a Greek-Persian-occult casserole and challenge the apostles' gospel.

Fifty years after John's death these semi-Christian hybrids were as common and various as roses, but the seeds were planted in John's lifetime. Many of the full-blown systems of the second century AD are grouped under the label *Gnosticism* (from the Greek *gnosis*, meaning "knowledge") because they all offered some secret knowledge by which a person could be saved. This knowledge was not available through study, but only through "revelation from a higher plane."[4] Gnosticism "is a religion of saving knowledge, and the knowledge is essentially self-knowledge, recognition of the divine element which constitutes the true self."[5]

Gnostics believe that matter is evil and spirit is good. Therefore, the world and the human body are also evil. They were created not by the Absolute (who is perfect), but by a lesser, malevolent spirit. We humans were all originally sublime spirit beings, but through no fault of our own we became imprisoned in physical bodies in this material world, ignorant of our lost bliss. Our only hope is for someone to redeem us by bringing that forgotten knowledge of our true natures. When a person learns what he was, what he

11

is, and what he can be, "that knowledge in itself becomes his redemption."[6]

Many variations on this theme were promoted in the second century AD. Some Gnostics identified the redeemer with Jesus. Others did not. Those that did talk of "Christ" were not thinking of the Jewish Messiah (*Christ* and *Messiah* both mean "Anointed One"—a Jewish king). They thought the Christ was an *aeon* (a sort of spirit) who had "emanated" from "the divine Absolute." Also, they differed over the relation between the Christ and Jesus. One group, called *Docetists* (from the Greek *dokein,* "to seem"), believed that Jesus was the Christ but only seemed to have a flesh-and-blood body. He was really a pure spirit being appearing visibly, as the angel of the Lord did in the Old Testament. To the Docetists, it was unthinkable for the divine Christ to be defiled by a material body.

We know of one teacher with Gnostic-like views who was busy in Ephesus while John lived there. He was Cerinthus, an Egyptian Jew. One of John's disciples told the story that

> John, the disciple of the Lord, going to bathe at Ephesus, and perceiving Cerinthus within, rushed out of the bath-house without bathing, exclaiming "Let us fly, lest even the bath-house fall down, because Cerinthus, the enemy of the truth, is within!"[7]

Why did the apostle so abhor Cerinthus? Because, wrote Irenaeus of Lyons (around 185 AD), Cerinthus

> represented Jesus as having not been born of a virgin, but as being the son of Joseph and Mary according to the ordinary course of human generation, while he nevertheless was more righteous, prudent and wise than other men. Moreover, after his baptism, Christ, descended upon him in the form of a dove from the Supreme Ruler, and that then he proclaimed the unknown Father, and performed miracles. But at last Christ departed from Jesus, and that then Jesus suffered and rose again, while Christ remained impassible [not liable to pain or injury] inasmuch as he was a spiritual being.[8]

Thus, Cerinthus said Jesus was a man, but the Christ was never incarnate— He only briefly occupied Jesus' body. This is just the kind of teaching John wrote his first epistle to deny (2:22, 4:2-3).

The letter suggests that some men with views like Cerinthus' joined the churches of Asia for a time and provoked strife with their unorthodox views. They eventually withdrew in anger when they failed to persuade the majority (2:19, 3:12-15), but the believers were upset. John probably wrote his letter to circulate among the troubled churches and calm the members.

---

1. Many scholars doubt the apostle wrote the letter. These include C. H. Dodd, Rudolf Bultmann, C. K. Barrett, and Raymond Brown, among many others. See, for example, Raymond E. Brown, *The Epistles of John* (Garden City, New York: Doubleday and Company, 1982). Others offer strong cases that he did write it. For specifics, see J. R. W. Stott, *The Epistles of John* (Grand Rapids, Michigan: William B. Eerdmans Publishing Company, 1964), pages 13-41; Leon Morris, *Studies in the Fourth Gospel* (Grand Rapids: William B. Eerdmans Publishing Company, 1969), pages 215-292; Leon Morris, *Commentary on the Gospel of John*

(Grand Rapids: William B. Eerdmans Publishing Company, 1971), pages 8-30; J. A. T. Robinson, *Redating the New Testament* (Philadelphia: Westminster Press, 1976), pages 254-311; Donald Burdick, *The Letters of John the Apostle* (Chicago: Moody Press, 1985), pages 7-37.

2. Our information about John's life comes mainly from the second-century bishop Irenaeus of Lyons and from the fourth-century church historian Eusebius of Caesarea. Their sources were oral traditions passed down from bishop to bishop.

3. Burdick, pages 38-44.

4. Burdick, page 55.

5. Robert M. Grant, *Gnosticism and Early Christianity* (New York: Columbia University Press, 1959), page 10. Technically, "Gnostic" applies to the full-blown systems that grew up after John's death. For simplicity, we will call John's opponents "Gnostics," rather than using the awkward term "proto-Gnostic."

6. Burdick, page 55.

7. Irenaeus, *Against Heresies*, in The Ante-Nicene Fathers, edited by Alexander Roberts and James Donaldson (Grand Rapids, Michigan: William B. Eerdmans Publishing Company, 1950), book 3, chapter 3, section 4. Irenaeus got the story from his mentor Polycarp, who was a disciple of John.

8. Irenaeus, *Against Heresies*, book 1, chapter 26, section 1.

LESSON ONE

OVERVIEW OF 1 JOHN

When you receive a letter from someone, how do you begin examining it? If you are like most people, you probably start by reading the whole letter through to get a general idea of what the writer has to say. You pay attention to the main ideas and feelings the sender is communicating, and you are alert for sections that you want to look at more closely later.

This is just the way to begin studying a biblical letter. First John is God's Word, but He chose to give us this information through a letter from an ordinary man to an ordinary group of Christians. Later you will want to think about what God is saying to you through this letter, but for now, imagine that you are one of John's original readers receiving this letter from a respected friend. Take about fifteen to thirty minutes to read through 1 John, not stopping to ponder phrases but scanning for the total message. If possible, read it twice in different translations. Read at least part of the letter aloud so that you can hear as well as see it. You can jot notes for questions 1 through 3 as you read or afterward.

1. What attitudes and feelings toward his readers does John show? (Also, how does he show his feelings?)

_____

_____

_____

For Thought and Discussion: Is John writing to Christians or nonChristians? How can you tell?

15

For Thought and Discussion: a. How would you describe John's *style* of writing? (Does he reason logically from point to point? Is there an obvious way to outline his letter?)

b. How is John's style like and unlike Paul's way of writing letters?

c. From the way he writes, what do you think John is like?

_____

_____

_____

2. Repetition is a clue to the ideas a writer wants to emphasize, and John makes especially strong use of this technique. List as many as possible of the key words, phrases, and ideas he repeats.

_____

_____

_____

_____

_____

_____

Study Skill—Broad Outline

To trace the train of thought in a biblical book, it is often helpful to sketch a general outline of it during your overview. On your first reading, notice where the writer's thought shifts, and mark the major sections of the book. Then, go back and give each section a title that expresses what it is about (see question 3). Key phrases in the section may give you clues to good titles.

3. You might find it difficult to decide for certain where John changes topics in his letter. He often seems to flow imperceptibly from one idea to the next. So, to help you make a broad outline of 1 John, we've chosen some rather arbitrary places to break the letter into sections. Make up a title or short summary for each passage. (You can change the divisions if you like.)

1:1-4 _____

_____

1:5-2:11 _____
_____

2:12-14 _____
_____

2:15-17 _____
_____

2:18-27 _____
_____

2:28-3:10 _____
_____

3:11-24 _____
_____

4:1-6 _____
_____

4:7-5:5 _____
_____

5:6-12 _____
_____

5:13-21 _____
_____

For Thought and Discussion: a. In what ways does John sound like a "Son of Thunder" in his letter?
b. What other aspects of his character balance this one?

4. What does John say about certain other people (not his readers)? Who are they, how does he feel about them, and why? (See, for instance, 2:18-26.)

_____
_____
_____
_____

_____

_____

_____

_____

5. Two of the ideas John repeats are what we may have *confidence* about and what we *know* for certain. In what may we have confidence (3:21, 4:17, 5:14)?

_____

_____

_____

_____

6. Over and over, John emphasizes *what* we know and *how* we can be certain that we know it. From the following verses, write down what we know and what tests assure us.

what we know	how we can be certain that we know this
2:3	
3:10	
3:14	

what we know	how we can be certain that we know this
3:24, 4:13	
5:1,11-13	

For Thought and Discussion: John is especially fond of contrasts. One example is light versus darkness. What other contrasts do you observe in his letter?

Study Skill—Themes and Purposes

People normally write letters in response to some situation in their own or their readers' lives. They usually have reasons for choosing the topics they cover in their letters. Although it is often not possible to reconstruct the precise reasons that prompted a letter, any insight in this area will help us understand a writer's message.

Our own purpose for studying a letter will often be different from its original purpose, but how we understand and apply a writer's words should be influenced by how he and the Holy Spirit meant them to be understood and applied in the first century. A clear idea of what we think John's letter is about, even if we have to modify it later, is a better foundation than a vague one.

---

7. What four purposes does John state in the following verses?

1:4 _____

_____

2:1 _____

_____

19

For Thought and Discussion: a. Gnostics believe that we are saved by knowing the truth about the world and ourselves. How is Christianity different?

b. Do you know of any modern groups with views like the Gnostics? What do they believe about Christ? About spirit and matter? About the origin of evil? About whether humans are divine? About how to "become who you are"?

c. Do you know any people who want to mix Christianity with other philosophies and religions?

2:26 _____

_____

_____

5:13 _____

_____

_____

8. From your first reading of John's letter, how would you summarize its main themes or purposes?

_____

_____

_____

_____

_____

9. If you have not already done so, read the Introduction on pages 9-13. If you feel you would like more background about 1 John, you might write your questions here. Some of your questions may be answered later in this study; the sources on pages 143-147 may answer others.

_____

_____

_____

_____

10. Your overview of 1 John may have suggested questions about particular passages that you would like to pursue as you go deeper into the book. If so, jot them down now while your thoughts are still fresh. Your questions can serve as personal objectives for your further investigation.

_____

_____

_____

_____

_____

_____

Optional Application: Take five or ten minutes to think and pray about 5:13. What difference would deep, confident knowledge of eternal life make to the way you deal with your circumstances? What difference would it make to the way you feel about yourself, God, and other people? Thank God for the opportunity to develop confidence about this, and ask Him to implant this confidence in you as you study John's letter.

Study Skill—Application

James 1:22 and 2 Timothy 3:16-17 remind us of the primary reason we study God's Word—to let it affect our lives so that we will fully become the people God desires. Therefore, the last step of Bible study should always be to ask yourself, "What is God saying to me? What difference should this passage make to my life? How should it make me want to think or act?" Application will require time, thought, prayer, and perhaps even discussion with another person.

At times you may find it most productive to concentrate on one specific application, giving it careful thought and prayer. At other times you may want to list many implications a passage of Scripture has for your life, meditating on them all for several days before you choose one for concentrated prayer and action. Use whatever method helps you to take to heart and act on what the passage says.

11. Think about the purposes you wrote in questions 7 and 8. How are any of them relevant or important to your life?

_____

_____

_____

_____

_____

_____

_____

21

12. Is there some part of John's letter that you
    would like to think and pray about this week, or
    something you want to act on? If so, describe
    your plans.

_____

_____

_____

_____

_____

_____

For the group

This "For the group" section and the ones in later
lessons are intended to suggest ways of structuring
your discussions. Feel free to select and adapt what
suits your group. The main goals are to get to know
1 John as a whole and the people with whom you
are going to study it.

Worship. Most groups like to begin with some kind
of worship—a few minutes of prayer and/or a cou-
ple of songs. Worship helps people lay aside the business of the day and focus on God. It relaxes, re-
news, and opens you to listen to the Lord and each
other. If you don't already have worship built into
your meetings in some way, discuss how you might
do so.

Warm-up. The beginning of a new study is a good
time to lay a foundation for honest sharing of ideas,
to get comfortable with each other, and to encourage a sense of common purpose. One way to estab-
lish common ground is to talk about what each
group member hopes to get out of your group—out
of any prayer, singing, sharing, outreach, or anything else you might do together. Why do you want
to study 1 John? What do you hope to give as well
as receive? If you have someone write down each
member's hopes and expectations, then you can
look back at these goals later to see if they are being
met.

How to use this study. If the group has never used a LIFECHANGE study guide before, you might take a whole meeting to discuss your goals for the group and go over the "How to Use This Study" section on pages 5-8. Then you can take a second meeting to talk about the background on pages 9-13 and the overview questions. This will give you more time to read 1 John and prepare lesson one for discussion.

Reading. It is often helpful to refresh everyone's memory by reading aloud the passage you are going to study. You probably won't want to read all of 1 John, but consider having someone read, for instance, 1:1-4, another read 1:5-2:2, and another 4:7-21. These selections will remind the group of John's themes, his style, and his personality.

First impressions. Ask the group to share first impressions of John's letter—its style, mood, content, or whatever strikes you. For instance, how is 1 John like and unlike letters group members write or receive, or like and unlike a sermon, a graduation speech, or advice from a father? What is John like as a person? How does he feel about his readers and about certain other people? What are his main topics? Help the group see 1 John as a real letter from a person to real people for some specific purposes.

The background on pages 9-13 should help you understand the setting of 1 John. Ask the group to describe the connections among *syncretism*, early *Gnosticism*, and what John has to say.

When you apply John's words, you'll have to transfer them from that first-century setting to your own. What signs of syncretism (mixing of religions and value systems) and Gnostic-like ideas do you observe in your day? What are some general ways in which John's words are relevant today? In what specific ways might you take to heart something he says? Encourage the group to pray about how the epistle applies to each of you personally. If some members are not used to purposefully applying a passage to themselves, take time at this or your next meeting to make up a sample application of some part of 1 John. The Study Skill on page 32 gives one example.

When you cover question 3, remind everyone that there is no one right way to title a passage. Compare and discuss the merits of different titles.

23

Questions. Give everyone a chance to share questions about the letter or the study guide. It is good to clear up confusion as early as possible. You may want to leave some questions about the book until later in your study; they may answer themselves if you are looking for answers. Point out the list of references on pages 143-147, and encourage members to bring questions to their pastors or other Christians they respect.

Outline. First John is not an easy book to outline, for John weaves topics together and flows from idea to idea. Therefore, many different outlines have been made. You may want to find several to compare from study Bibles, commentaries, and Bible handbooks. Here is one example:[1]

I. Introduction: The Reality of the Incarnation (1:1-4)
II. The Christian Life as Fellowship with the Father and the Son (1:5-2:28)
   A. Ethical Tests of Fellowship (1:5-2:11)
   B. Two Digressions (2:12-17)
   C. Christological Test of Fellowship (2:18-28)
III. The Christian Life as Divine Sonship (2:29-4:6)
   A. Ethical Tests of Sonship (2:29-3:24)
   B. Christological Test of Sonship (4:1-6)
IV. The Christian Life as an Integration of the Ethical and the Christological (4:7-5:12)
   A. The Ethical Test: Love (4:7-5:5)
   B. The Christological Test (5:6-12)
V. Conclusion: Great Christian Certainties (5:13-21)

Wrap-up. The group leader should have read lesson two and its "For the group" section. At this point, he or she can give a short summary of what members can expect in that lesson and the coming meeting. This is a chance to whet everyone's appetite, assign any optional questions, omit or clarify any numbered questions, or forewarn members of any possible difficulties.

You might also encourage anyone who found the overview especially hard. Some people are better at seeing the big picture or the whole of a book than others. Some are best at analyzing a particular verse or paragraph, while others are strongest at seeing how a passage applies to our lives. Urge

24

members to give thanks for their own and others'
strengths, and to give and request help when
needed. The group is a place to learn from each
other. Later lessons will draw on the gifts of close
analyzers as well as overviewers and appliers, practical as well as theoretical thinkers.

Worship. Many groups like to end with singing
and/or prayer. This can include songs and prayers
that respond to what you've learned from 1 John, or
prayers for specific needs of group members. Many
people are shy about sharing personal needs or praying aloud in groups, especially before they know the
other people well. If this is true of your group, then
a song and/or some silent prayer, and a short clos-
ing prayer by the leader, might be an appropriate
end. You could share requests and pray in pairs
instead.

1. Adapted from Burdick, pages 88-90. Burdick thinks the letter
   covers the tests of real Christianity in three ever-deepening
   cycles.

1 JOHN 1:1-4

The Word of Life

*"We proclaim to you the eternal life, which was
with the Father and has appeared to us."*
1 John 1:2

Most letters of John's day begin like those Paul
writes, following the form: "Person A to Person B:
Greetings" (see Acts 15:23 or 2 John 1). However,
John doesn't state his own name or titles, nor does
he say who his readers are. Instead, he begins with a
preface that reminds us of the prologue to his Gospel. Read 1 John 1:1-4 and John 1:1-4, and think
about why the apostle begins his letter as he does.
Ask God to enlighten your mind and heart as you
study this passage.

1. In the original Greek, 1:1-3 is all one sentence.
   The subject and verb don't appear until verse 3
   (although the NIV adds it to verse 1 for clarity).
   The subject and verb are "we proclaim." What
   does John proclaim in 1:1-3?

   _____

   _____

   _____

   _____

   _____

   _____

For Thought and Discussion: How is the idea of Jesus being your eternal life different from reincarnation or other ideas of eternal life you have heard?

For Further Study: Compare 1 John 1:2 to the way Jesus defines eternal life in John 17:3.

From the beginning (1:1). The beginning of all things, as in Genesis 1:1 and John 1:1.[1]

Word of life (1:1). Either Jesus or the gospel about Him. In John 1:1 the Word is Jesus, so some people think the Word is Jesus in 1 John 1:1. In that case, "the Word of life" means "the Word [Jesus] who is the life."[2]

However, 1 John 1:2 says, "the life appeared" and "we proclaim . . . the eternal life," not "the Word appeared" and "we proclaim . . . the Word." Therefore, some think "the life" is Jesus (as in John 11:25, 14:6) and "the Word of life" is the gospel about Jesus, who is the life.[3]

These are not necessarily exclusive views, since Jesus is both the Word and the Life.

2. John calls Jesus "the eternal life, which was with the Father and has appeared to us" (1:2). What does it imply about Jesus to call Him "the life"?

_____

_____

_____

_____

_____

_____

3. What does John insist is true about the life (Jesus) in 1:1-3?

_____

_____

_____

_____

_____

_____

28

4. Why is it crucial that "the life appeared" to men and women on earth (1:2)?

_____

_____

_____

_____

_____

_____

For Thought and Discussion: A witness is qualified to testify only about what he knows firsthand. No one alive today is an eyewitness to the Resurrection; the New Testament is our eyewitness testimony. However, what are you qualified to testify about concerning the Word of life?

Eternal (1:2). The Greek word *aionion* means "belonging to the age to come" and "belonging to eternity." In the latter sense it describes an unending *quantity* of time. In the former sense it denotes the *quality* of life in the Kingdom of God—spiritual, abundant, glorious, divine.[4]

5. What difference does it make to you that Jesus is the eternal life? How should this fact affect your thoughts and actions?

_____

_____

_____

_____

_____

_____

Seen . . . looked at (1:1). The Greek word for "to see" is used three times in 1:1-3. However, 1 John 1:1 also uses a word which means "to scrutinize," "to inspect carefully," or "to examine intelligently."

Testify . . . proclaim (1:2-3). The former verb in verse 2 means "to bear witness." It implies that

29

For Thought and Discussion: Why does John stress his authority to proclaim his message (1:1)? Consider 2:18-19,26.

For Thought and Discussion: Why is it important that John was able to scrutinize and handle Jesus both before His crucifixion and after His resurrection (1:1)?

For Thought and Discussion: Why does John's complete joy depend on his readers understanding and embracing the message about Jesus?

the person is qualified because he is a firsthand witness of the events, not just reporting what others say.

The Greek word translated "proclaim" in verses 2 and 3 signifies "the authority of commission. . . . In order to witness, the apostles must have seen and heard Christ for themselves; in order to proclaim, they must have received a commission from Him."[5]

---

6. Why is John qualified to testify about what he proclaims? (Compare 1 John 1:1 to John 20:1-9,19-31. *Optional:* Consider other passages in the Gospels, such as Luke 5:1-11, 8:40-56, 9:28-36.)

_____

_____

_____

_____

_____

_____

_____

7. John gives two connected reasons why he is proclaiming his message to his readers. What are his reasons?

1:3 _____

_____

_____

_____

1:4 _____

_____

_____

_____

Fellowship (1:3). *Koinonia* means "a joint participation in a common interest or activity."[6] It is the usual Greek word for a business partnership, common ownership, or participation in a community. There is a different Greek word for passive sharing, but *koinonia* is active.[7] Because Christians share a common faith in Christ, they also share a common relationship with God and each other, as well as a common mission. To be a Christian is to be "in Christ" and "united with Christ," and to share "the fellowship of the Holy Spirit" with others who are also "in Christ."

For Thought and Discussion: a. What would John say to a person who believed that the historical Jesus (who was born and walked on the earth) is different from the Christ of faith (whom we pray to and trust for salvation)?

b. What would he say to someone who thinks that the supernatural, spiritual world either doesn't exist or isn't involved with the natural, physical world?

8. Accepting John's message about Jesus puts people into fellowship with God and each other. What evidence of that fellowship can you observe in your own experiences and actions?

fellowship with God _____

_____

_____

_____

fellowship with other believers _____

_____

_____

_____

_____

Study Skill—Summarizing

It's often helpful to summarize a passage in some way after you've studied it, so you can remember it better. You can summarize it in a sentence, or make up a title that expresses what it is about. If you look for key phrases from the passage, they can often help you make a title or summary.

For Thought and Discussion: Is it possible to have true fellowship with people who deny that Jesus is the eternal Son of God? Why or why not?

Optional Application: This week, meditate on the fact that Jesus is life. (Do you really want life? Do you seek life from other sources besides Jesus? If you are glad to have life, how do you show it? If you are not glad, should you be honest about this?) Ask God to help you understand what it means to you that Jesus is life, and to enable you to act on this knowledge.

9. Summarize 1:1-4 in a sentence or title. Use the title of this lesson and the one in the outline on page 24 as examples.

_____

_____

_____

_____

_____

Study Skill—Application

It can be helpful to plan an application in five steps:

1. Record the verse or passage that contains the truth you want to apply to your life. If the passage is short enough, consider copying it word for word, as an aid to memory. (Memorizing the passage is always a good idea, since you can then meditate on it anytime during the day.)

2. State the truth of the passage that impresses you. For instance, *"Jesus is eternal life who became human flesh."*

3. Describe how you already see this truth at work positively in your life. (This is a chance to rejoice in what God is doing.) For example, *"Knowing Jesus has made me feel really alive—full of energy and purpose—for the first time. I know I'm plugged into real life at last."*

4. Tell how you fall short in relation to this truth, or how you want the truth to affect your life. (Ask God to enable you to see yourself clearly.) For example, *"I have a tendency sometimes to flee from life into my protective shell, and sometimes to make a pretense of living on my own, without Jesus. If I want to live fully, understand life, and not be just a walking corpse, I have to know and be intimately connected to Jesus."*

5. State precisely what you plan to do about having your life changed in this area. (Ask God what, if anything, you can do. Don't

(continued on page 33)

(continued from page 32)

forget that transformation depends on His will, power, and timing, not on yours. Diligent prayer should always be part of your application.) For instance, *"I'm going to meditate on 1 John 1:1-2 for five or ten minutes each day this week. I'm going to copy those verses and tape them on my desk to remind myself. I'm going to ask God to forgive me for fleeing from life and for trying to live on my own. I'll ask Him also to enable me to experience the life of Jesus firsthand this week. I'll spend time each morning just being with Jesus, and I'll keep inviting Him to be with me during the day. Every day I'll thank God for giving me the life of Jesus."*

6. Plan a way to remind yourself to do what you've decided, such as putting a note on your refrigerator or in your office, or asking a friend to remind you.[8]

Optional Application: Pray about your fellowship with God and others. How do you already reflect partnership in your thoughts and actions? How could you show it better? Talk with some other Christians about how you could put fellowship into practice. (If you like, look up other references to fellowship, partnership, and participation in the New Testament, using a concordance.)

10. a. What truth from 1:1-4 would you like to take to heart this week?

_____

_____

_____

_____

_____

_____

b. How do you already see this truth affecting your life?

_____

_____

_____

_____

_____

c. How do you fall short or want to grow in this area?

_____

_____

_____

_____

_____

_____

d. What can you do to cooperate with God in producing this growth?

_____

_____

_____

_____

_____

_____

e. How can you make sure you will do what you have planned?

_____

_____

_____

_____

11. If you have any questions about 1:1-4 or the material in this lesson, record them here.

_____

_____

_____

_____

_____

For the group

Worship.

Warm-up. To help the group focus on the topic at hand, it's often a good idea to begin with a warm-up question that connects the topic to people's daily lives. For example, you could begin this meeting by asking, "What are some of the things you have seen and handled (your personal experiences) that are part of the basis of your faith? What would you say if you were asked why you believe the gospel?" You are more concerned with sparking interest, involvement, and familiarity with each other than with getting thorough answers. The more you know one another, the deeper your sharing of applications and "fellowship" will be.

Read aloud. Ask someone to read 1:1-4 aloud with as much expression as possible. Suggest that the reader first think for a moment about the mood or emotion John wanted to convey.

Summarize. Before you start analyzing phrases, step back and summarize what 1:1-4 is about. Question 9 may help. You don't need a perfect, comprehensive summary at this stage. You'll summarize the passage again after studying it in detail.

Questions. Never feel that you must cover all the questions in a Bible study lesson just because they are in the book. You can focus on one or two concepts, or ignore the numbered questions and discuss some optional questions that interest you. For instance, concentrate on one or two of these issues raised in 1:1-4:

> Jesus is life (What does this mean? What does it imply for your lives?)
>
> John's authority (What kind of authority does he claim? What qualifies him to claim it? Why does he stress his authority? What difference does it make to you?)
>
> Jesus is both divine and a physical person (Why was this important to John? Why is it important to you?)
>
> Fellowship (What is it? How do you obtain and maintain it? How are you experiencing it, or not experiencing it? How does having fellowship affect what you think and do?)

Background notes. The study guide is full of word definitions and comments on the text. Don't get bogged down in these; you don't have to learn it all. Feel free to discuss and/or disagree with the notes. When alternate interpretations (such as for "the Word of life" and "we") are given, you might discuss which view convinces you.

Application. Give everyone a chance to share his or her plans for applying 1:1-4. If necessary, help each other think of specific ways to act on a truth John states. If some of you don't feel any action is appropriate, do at least plan to meditate and pray about something in the passage this week. This gives God a chance to transform your attitudes and lead you into situations for active application. Urge everyone to come to your next meeting ready to share results, insights, experiences, and even failures in applying 1:1-4.

Fellowship means partly that each of you in the group is responsible to pray for and encourage the rest (5:16 is just one way among many). Ask the group to look for ways of fostering partnership among yourselves. Ask everyone to pray for the other members this week.

Summarize. Now that you've studied 1:1-4 together, what do you think it is about? Summarize both the passage and how it applies to you.

Worship. Praise Jesus as the eternal life which was with the Father and appeared to the apostles. Thank the Father for your fellowship with Him, with His Son, and with each other. Ask Them to strengthen that fellowship by deepening your knowledge of and obedience to the Father and the Son.

1. Stott, pages 58-59.
2. Burdick, page 101.
3. Stott, pages 66-68.
4. Burdick, pages 102-103.
5. Stott, pages 61-62.
6. Kenneth Wuest, *Philippians in the Greek New Testament* (Grand Rapids, Michigan: William B. Eerdmans Publishing Company, 1942), page 31.
7. Burdick, pages 104-105.
8. This "Five-point Application" is based on the method in *The 2:7 Series*, Course 4 (Colorado Springs: NavPress, 1979), pages 50-51.

1 JOHN 1:5-2:2

The Light

"God is light; in him there is no darkness at all."
1 John 1:5

The apostles proclaim their message, says John, in order that we may share in their fellowship with the Father and the Son (1:3). However, some false apostles are abroad teaching an altered message and thereby threatening fellowship. Against that threat, John declares in the strongest terms what the apostles received from Jesus and what that means for our lives.

Before you begin the questions below, read 1:5-2:2. Then look back at question 3 on page 17 to recall the title you gave 1:5-2:11. Ask God to reveal Himself to you through the passage you are about to study.

Light (1:5). See the box, "Light and Darkness," on page 46.

1. John announces what he heard from Jesus: "God is light" (1:5). What do you think this statement means?

_____

_____

_____

For Thought and Discussion: a. Compare the three false claims in question 2 to the Gnostic beliefs about sin described on page 46.

b. Do any modern groups have views like those you wrote in question 2?

_____

_____

_____

_____

Study Skill—Parallelism

If you've read the Old Testament much, you are familiar with the Hebrew habit of pairing statements that intensify each other, showing different facets of the same truth (Isaiah 44:3-4 is an example). John does this frequently in his letter. For example, in 1:5 he does not just say "God is light"; he adds, "in him there is no darkness at all." Watch for this element of style, and think about what the parallel statements add to each other.

2. Three times in 1:5-2:2, John says "if we claim . . ." to introduce a belief he thinks is false. These are probably doctrines of the teachers he wants to refute. What are those three false claims?

1:6 _____

_____

_____

1:8 _____

_____

_____

1:10 _____

_____

_____

Walking in the light (1:5-7)

3. According to 1:5-6, why is it a lie to claim fellowship with God if we "walk" (live habitually)

38

in "darkness" (wickedness, error)? (Remember from page 31 what fellowship really is.)

_____

_____

_____

_____

_____

Study Skill—Interpretation

Phrases like "God is light" and "if we walk in the light" aren't obvious. They have to be interpreted. On the one hand, don't feel you must come up with the perfect, exhaustive definition. Your insight will grow as you mature in Christ. On the other hand, some interpretations are more right than others (some, of course, are wrong), so do think carefully and take the rest of Scripture into account as much as possible.

4. To have fellowship with God and each other, we must walk with Him in the light (1:7). In your judgment, what does it mean to walk in the light?

_____

_____

_____

_____

_____

Confessing sin (1:8-2:2)

5. What does a person walking in the light still need from Jesus (1:7)?

_____

_____

For Thought and Discussion: a. What would John say to someone who claims, "I used to have a sinful nature and commit sins, but now Jesus has cleansed me and I no longer ever sin"? Why would he agree or disagree?

b. Do you know any groups who believe this?

For Thought and Discussion: Is it possible to be walking in the light and confessing sin without spending lots of time with God? Why or why not?

For Further Study: How does Jesus' blood cleanse us from sin (1:7)? See 1 John 2:2; Hebrews 9:1-14, 10:1-18; Leviticus 16:1-22.

For Thought and Discussion: The person who claims fellowship with God while walking in darkness is lying; he knows this is false (1:6). However, the one who claims to be sinless is self-deceived (1:8). Why does John make this distinction?

_____

_____

_____

Sin (1:7). *Hamartia* is a term from archery that means "missing the mark." To sin is to miss the mark of God's standard for us: glory (Romans 3:23) or being like Jesus (Romans 8:29, 1 John 3:2). Another definition of sin is in 1 John 3:4.

6. How can we be walking in the light even though we still need purification from sin (1:7-8)? (Consider what walking in the light means if it doesn't mean never sinning.)

_____

_____

_____

_____

_____

7. Since we aren't sinless even if we walk in the light, what must we keep doing (1:9)?

_____

_____

_____

_____

_____

Confess (1:9). Literally, "to say the same as." We agree with God regarding His standards and our failures.

Faithful and just (1:9). God's faithfulness is related to His covenant promises (Psalm 89, Hebrews

10:23). "He is true to His word and faithful to His covenant. Since the new covenant includes the pledge, 'I will forgive their iniquity, and I will remember their sin no more' (Jeremiah 31:34, RSV), it is not difficult to see why God is said to be 'faithful' in forgiving our sins."[1]

If God is just, it would seem that He should punish our sins, not forgive them. But "the blood of Jesus, his Son, purifies us from all sin" (1 John 1:7). In His death, Jesus bore the just penalty for our sin, so God is righteous in acquitting us (Romans 3:25-26).

For Thought and Discussion: What is the connection between walking in the light and confessing sin?

Optional Application: Meditate on the fact that God is both faithful and just. He shows this by forgiving your sins; how else does He show it? Ask Him to fully convince you of this truth and to teach you how to respond to His faithfulness and justice. What difference should these facts about God make to your life?

8. Why does denying that we have sinned make God out to be a liar (1:10)? (*Optional:* See what God's Word says in 1 Kings 8:46, Ecclesiastes 7:20, Isaiah 53:6.)

_____

_____

_____

_____

For Thought and Discussion: What does John say about righteousness and unrighteousness in 1:9 and 2:1?

One who speaks to the Father in our defense (2:1). "An Advocate" in KJV, RSV, NASB. The Greek word means "one called alongside" to help in some way. It was used mainly of a friend who testified to the good character of a person on trial. The word occurs in Scripture only in John's writings. Here it refers to Jesus pleading for us in heaven, but in John 14:16,26; 15:26; and 16:7 it refers to the Holy Spirit advocating Christ's cause on earth.[2] The Spirit argues for Jesus on the grounds that He is righteous, but Jesus argues for us on the grounds that although we are guilty, He has paid our penalty. He is qualified to bear the punishment in our stead because He is *the Righteous One*.

Atoning sacrifice (2:2, 4:10). "Propitiation" in KJV, NASB; "expiation" in RSV. The pagan Greeks used this word for an offering that appeased an angry god. The Greek gods were not perfectly

41

Optional Application: What difference does it make to you that you have an Advocate with the Father?

For Thought and Discussion: What does the need for propitiation and atonement tell you about God and yourself?

moral and loving, but capricious and sometimes cruel to those who aroused their ire. However, the Father of Jesus is justly angry with man because of man's rebellion and depravity. But because He grieves to be angry at His creatures, He Himself has provided the sacrifice that *propitiates* Him (satisfies the justice of His wrath).

In His death, Jesus *expiated* (removed) our guilt from us and took it on Himself. Then, the death of Jesus *atoned for* (covered) our sin by substituting the death of an innocent victim for the death of the guilty persons. This principle of substitution lay behind the whole Old Testament sacrificial system (Leviticus 4:13-21, 16:1-22). Hebrews 9:24-28 explains this.[3]

For the sins of the whole world (2:2). In what sense is Jesus the atonement for the whole world? Several answers have been offered:

1. Every human being is saved by His sacrifice and will be in heaven. (However, elsewhere John distinguishes sharply between those who belong to Christ and those who belong to the world [John 13:1; 17:9; 1 John 3:1,10]. Full universalism just doesn't square with the rest of the New Testament.)

2. Forgiveness through Christ's death is available to every person, but it is effective only if a person appropriates it by faith.

3. Unlike the Old Testament offerings and the Day of Atonement (Leviticus 16), Christ's sacrifice applies to Gentiles as well as Jews—the whole world from John's Jewish point of view.[4]

9. In case 1:7-10 gives anyone the impression that it is okay for Christians to sin, John adds 2:1-2 as a parenthesis.

a. How does John avoid being too lenient with sin (1:5-6; 2:1,3-6)?

_____

_____

_____

_____

_____

_____

_____

b. How does he avoid being too severe with
sinners (1:7-9, 2:1-2)?

_____

_____

_____

_____

_____

**Optional
Application:** Explain
in your own words
what Christ has done
and is doing for you
(1:7, 2:1-2). What dif-
ference should His
deeds make to the
way you think and
act?

10. Now that you've studied 1:5-2:2 carefully, reread
the passage and summarize it in a sentence or
title.

_____

_____

_____

_____

_____

Study Skill—Application
When you're looking for a truth in a passage
to apply to yourself, consider the following
five questions:
    Is there a *sin* for me to avoid?
    Is there a *promise* for me to trust?
    Is there an *example* for me to follow?
    Is there a *command* for me to obey?
    How can this passage increase my
knowledge of the Lord (not just knowledge
about Him)?
    You can recall these five questions by
remembering the acronym SPECK—Sin,
Promise, Example, Command, Knowledge.

Optional Application: Meditate on the fact that God is light and on what this implies for your actions (1:5-7). Praise God for being light, and ask Him to reveal Himself to you as light while you spend time with Him.

11. Is there any insight from 1:5-2:2 that you would like to concentrate on this week? If so, write it down.

_____

_____

_____

_____

_____

_____

12. How do you see it already at work in your life?

_____

_____

_____

_____

13. How would you like to grow in this area?

_____

_____

_____

_____

14. What can you do to accomplish this, by God's grace?

_____

_____

_____

_____

15. List any questions you have about 1:5-2:2.

_____

_____

_____

_____

Optional Application: Prayerfully make a list of what you can do to walk in the light this week. Review and add to your list every morning. Be alert during the day for failings you need to confess. Each evening, ask God to help you walk in the light the next day.

For the group

Warm-up. Ask group members if they have been aware of close fellowship with God today. Also ask, "Why or why not, do you think?" Feelings can be a deceptive measure of closeness to God. In this lesson you'll be discussing some of John's objective measures of fellowship—walking in the light and confessing sin. Still, sharing how each person assesses his current walk with God can help you get to know each other. This warm-up may also raise topics for you to pray about at the end of your meeting.

Read aloud.

Questions. The two key concepts are _walking in the light_ and _what Jesus does for those who confess sin_. Does walking in the light mean sinless perfection? Why or why not? Why must Jesus keep cleansing us and interceding for us? Why does our fellowship depend on these things?

Application. Give everyone a chance to share joys and frustrations from the last lesson's applications. What prayer, encouragement, or counsel would any member like from the group? Then discuss specific ways of applying 1:5-2:2.

Summarize.

Worship. Praise God for being light. Meditate together on what that means and what it implies for your lives. Thank Jesus for being your propitiation and your Advocate. Ask Him to enable you to walk in the light. You might plan time to pray and confess (silently or aloud) any sins weighing on members of the group. Thank God for being faithful and just to forgive and cleanse.

Light and Darkness

All the religious traditions surrounding John and his readers had symbolisms of light and darkness, but they did not all agree. John followed the Old Testament, while his opponents had pre-Gnostic views. We can see similar differences today between biblical and nonbiblical faiths.

"Intellectually, light is truth and darkness ignorance or error" in Scripture. "Morally, light is purity and darkness evil."[5] Psalm 119:105,130 and Proverbs 6:23 describe God's revelation and commandments as light that shows both the true way things are and the true way to live. Because light is essential to life, it becomes a symbol of life and darkness of death.

Light is also a major way in which God manifests Himself (Psalm 104:2, Habakkuk 3:4). "The LORD is my light and my salvation," says the Psalmist (Psalm 27:1; compare Job 22:28). However, Scripture insists that light is a *metaphor* for God's purity, truth, and revelation to man; physical light is created by God, and He is greater than both light and darkness (Genesis 1:3-5,14-19).

By contrast, the Gnostics saw light and darkness as truth and error, but not as moral purity and wickedness. Man is in the darkness of ignorance, so he "needs to liberate the elements of light within his own soul, and free them from earthly matter so that they may be re-united with the supernatural world to which they really belong and so attain to true life."[6] Light represents life, the spirit, and true knowledge; darkness is death, the physical body, and ignorance. The moral element is absent, because "sin" for the Gnostic is simply ignorance. The person with the secret knowledge no longer has to worry about sin.

Persian religion saw light and darkness, good and evil, as two balanced aspects within God. This belief has become widespread in our day among religious groups with Eastern influence. It contradicts John's view that "God is light; in him there is no darkness at all" (1:5).

46

1. Stott, page 77.
2. Burdick, page 130.
3. Burdick, pages 78-79, 131-132; Stott, pages 81-88; Leon Morris, *The Apostolic Preaching of the Cross* (Grand Rapids, Michigan: William B. Eerdmans Publishing Company, 1965), pages 125-185, 205-207.
4. James Montgomery Boice, *The Epistles of John: An Expositional Commentary* (Grand Rapids, Michigan: Zondervan Corporation, 1979), pages 51-52.
5. Stott, page 71.
6. Hans-Christoph Hahn, "Light," *The New International Dictionary of New Testament Theology,* volume 2, edited by Colin Brown (Grand Rapids, Michigan: Zondervan Corporation, 1976), page 491.

1 JOHN 2:3-11

Ethical Tests

"We know that we have come to know him if we obey his commands."
1 John 2:3

Gnostics claim to know the truth and therefore to know God. Their sophisticated teaching makes some Christians begin to doubt that they know anything for certain, especially God. To encourage the faithful and refute the heretics, John states two tests by which a person can be sure of what he knows. The first test is *ethical*—we examine our actions to see what heart attitudes they reflect. John began to explain this in 1:5-2:2. As he continues in 2:3-11, keep in mind John's foundational proclamation—"God is light; in him there is no darkness at all" (1:5).

Study Skill—Outlining
First John is not easy to outline. Look at several commentaries and study Bibles, to find a variety of views. You might find them helpful as you try to flesh out the one you sketched in question 3 of lesson one (pages 16-17).

---

1. For practice in outlining, list the four ethical tests of fellowship with God (or four aspects of one test)[1] in 1:5-2:11.

   (1:5-7) Fellowship with God requires _____

For Thought and Discussion: Do you ever wonder whether you really know God? How can you be sure that you do?

For Thought and Discussion: How does 2:4 guide us in discerning which teachers of Christianity we should listen to? How can we decide who knows truth?

(1:8-2:2) Fellowship requires _____

_____

(2:3-6) Knowing and being "in" God require

_____

(2:7-11) Knowing God requires _____

_____

Obedience (2:3-6)

Know (2:3). John uses this word in two senses. To know a fact or the truth is primarily intellectual, although this knowledge needs to sink deep into our convictions before it consistently affects our thoughts and actions. On the other hand, to know God is to know a person. Knowledge in this sense is intimate and based on personal experience. It is used in Genesis 4:1 to describe relations between man and wife, and in Amos 3:2 for God's choice of a covenant people.

Obey (2:3). "Keep" in KJV. The Greek word "expresses the idea of watchful, observant obedience."[2]

2. Why is it a lie to claim to know God without obeying Him (2:4)? (*Optional:* See Exodus 34:5-8, Deuteronomy 10:14-22.)

_____

_____

_____

_____

_____

_____

3. In light of 1:8-10, does John mean that we know God only if we perfectly obey all His

50

commands? What does he mean, and why do you think so?

_____

_____

_____

_____

_____

_____

God's love (2:5). Literally, "the love of God." This could mean that God's love for us is made complete (brought to the fulfillment of its purpose) when it moves us to act obediently (4:12), or that our love for God "becomes complete when it expresses itself in acts of obedience"[3] (4:19-5:3).

Complete ("perfected" in NASB) doesn't mean that we have perfect, flawless love. Rather, obedience is the fulfillment, the completion, of love.

4. Why does obedience make the love of God perfect (complete, fulfilled) in a person (2:5)?

_____

_____

_____

_____

_____

5. How does John define obedience to God in 2:6?

_____

_____

_____

51

For Thought and Discussion: In what sense is the command of 2:7-8 an old one?

For Thought and Discussion: John emphasized love because Jesus did. Why do you think Jesus emphasized love? (See Matthew 22:34-40, Romans 13:8-10.)

For Thought and Discussion: How is the truth of the new command seen in Jesus and in you (2:8)? (See 3:16-18.)

Love (2:7-11)

Dear friends (2:7). Literally, "Beloved"—an appropriate address for this paragraph.

The true light (2:8). Primarily Jesus (John 1:9, 3:19). However, He who is the Light of the world makes us the light of the world by giving us the light of the gospel and the light of love (Matthew 5:14-16, John 8:12).

6. John has been writing about God's commands in general; now he discusses one in particular. What is the command that is both old and new (Leviticus 19:18, Matthew 22:34-40, John 13:34-35)?

_____

_____

_____

7. How has Jesus given the old command new meaning (John 15:12-13; 1 John 2:8, 3:16)?

_____

_____

_____

_____

_____

_____

Hates . . . loves (2:9-10). John favors strong contrasts, like light and darkness, truth and lies. Because love is primarily active, the lack of love is not neutral indifference, but hate.

John will explain what he thinks love is (3:11-18, 4:7-21). He does not use the common Greek words which mean fondness among friends and relatives (*phileo, philia*), affection

52

between parent and child (*stergo, storge*), or passion between lovers (*erao, eros*). Instead, he invariably uses the words Greek-speaking Jews chose to express the love between God and His covenant people—the verb *agapao* and the noun *agape*.[4]

While the other loves are based on warm feeling, *agape* is "an intelligent, purposeful attitude of esteem and devotion,"[5] "a selfless, purposeful, outgoing attitude that desires to do good to the one loved."[6] "In secular Greek it represented a love in which the mind analyzes and the will chooses the object to be loved. Thus it is not a term wholly given to emotion, but it involves the whole man, emotions, intellect, and will. *Agape* is a deliberate, free act that is the decision of the subject rather than the result of unbidden, overpowering emotion."[7]

For Thought and Discussion: What is hate? Why do people hate?

For Further Study: See what Jesus has to say about avoiding stumbling in John 11:9-10. How does this relate to 1 John 2:9-10?

Optional Application: Is there anyone whom you are failing to love, not because you hate them emotionally, but because you just don't care? Is there anyone you should love more actively? (Ask God about this.) If so, what should you do?

8. If a person loves his brother, "there is nothing in him to make him stumble" (2:10). What does this mean, and why is it so?

_____

_____

_____

_____

_____

_____

_____

_____

9. What happens to a person who hates (2:11)?

_____

_____

_____

_____

_____

53

Optional Application: Is any current or past hatred or unforgiveness blinding you (2:11)? If so, confess it, forgive, and be forgiven (1:8-10).

For Thought and Discussion: What is the connection between walking in the light and confessing sin? Between walking in the light and obeying God? Between walking in the light and loving your brother?

Obedience and love

10. What is wrong with trying to obey God's commandments (such as the Ten Commandments or Matthew 5-7) without love? (*Optional:* See Romans 13:8-10, 1 Corinthians 13:1-3.)

_____

_____

_____

_____

_____

_____

11. What is wrong with trying to love without obeying God's commandments? (*Optional:* See Matthew 5:17-20, John 14:15.)

_____

_____

_____

_____

_____

John explains the connection between love and obedience more fully later in his letter.

12. Summarize John's message in 2:3-11.

_____

_____

_____

_____

_____

_____

_____

13. Is there any truth in 2:3-11 that you would like to apply? If so, what is it?

_____

_____

_____

_____

_____

14. How is this truth already affecting your life?

_____

_____

_____

_____

_____

15. How do you fall short in this area, or how do you want to grow?

_____

_____

_____

_____

_____

16. If there is anything you can do to cooperate with God in accomplishing this, describe your plans.

_____

_____

_____

_____

_____

Optional Application: Are you disregarding any of God's commands? Read Exodus 20:1-17 or Matthew 5:1-7:27 prayerfully. If you find yourself convicted, apply 1 John 1:9, renounce your sin, and ask God to help you become free of it.

For Thought and Discussion:
a. Explain John's train of thought from 1:1-4 to 1:5-2:2 to 2:3-2:11.
   b. Outline 1:5-2:11.

17. List any questions you have about 2:3-11.

_____

_____

_____

_____

For the group

Warm-up. Share how your efforts to apply 1:5-2:2 are going. What have you learned about yourselves? What obstacles have you encountered, what successes have you had, or what questions have you been wondering about? Does anyone need prayer to be able to do what John says? Keep this discussion to about five or ten minutes so that it doesn't interfere with the current lesson.

Read aloud.

Summarize. Questions 1 and 12 are summary questions. Question 1 is tightly directive so as to help those who find summarizing and outlining difficult, while question 12 is open-ended to give freedom to more experienced students. Encourage confident people to make their own outlines, and urge the less confident to look at some outlines in study Bibles or handbooks.

Questions. Never feel obliged to discuss all of the questions in a lesson. Many of them are simple observations. If two or three discussion questions interest the group, you can spend your whole time on them. But stress application—how can each of you actively obey God and love some person this week? Help group members to be specific about what they plan to do. Model openness by confessing your own disobedience and lack of love. Tell how you want to change.

Pray for anyone who asks for prayer to be more obedient and loving in specific situations. Pray especially for those of you who feel unable to let go of some hate or unforgiveness, perhaps because of fear.

Worship. Confess your disobedience and lack of love. Thank God for forgiving you and atoning for your sins. Thank Him for His commandments and for enabling you to keep them by His power. Thank Him that the darkness is passing and the light is already shining. Pray for the ability and discipline to obey and love.

1. This outline follows the approach in Donald Burdick, *The Letters of John the Apostle.* John Stott distinguishes love as a separate test from obedience, whereas Burdick sees them as two aspects of one ethical test.
2. Robert Law, *The Tests of Life* (London: T. and T. Clark, 1909), quoted in Stott, page 90.
3. *The NIV Study Bible,* page 1909.
4. Walther Gunther and Hans-Georg Link, "Love," *The New International Dictionary of New Testament Theology,* volume 2, pages 538-547.
5. Burdick, page 177.
6. Burdick, page 284.
7. Burdick, page 140.

1 JOHN 2:12-17

Two Digressions

"The world and its desires pass away, but the man who does the will of God lives forever."
1 John 2:17

John has given his readers some tests to assure them that they really know God. His purpose is to encourage them, but after observing their own fitful obedience and puny love, some may decide that they fail the tests. So, before giving his final test, John pauses to reassure and caution his flock.

Read 2:12-17, looking for John's reassurance and warning.

I write to you (2:12-14)

1. Observe the pattern of John's words in 2:12-14. What is this paragraph about? (Look back at your title on page 17.)

_____

_____

_____

_____

_____

_____

_____

For Thought and Discussion: What two complimentary truths about forgiveness does John state in 1:8-10 and 2:12? Why are they both important to remember?

For Thought and Discussion: a. What basic experiences of Christian life can even babes in faith be certain of (2:12-13)? Why are these assurances especially important for new believers?

b. Why does John say that children know "the Father" (2:13)? See Galatians 4:6-7.

c. Why do you think he says mature Christians know "him who is from the beginning" (2:13-14)? How is this a deeper insight than knowing the Father?

d. How does John reassure growing Christians engaged in spiritual warfare against sin (2:13-14)? Why are these assurances especially significant for "young men"?

Dear children . . . fathers . . . young men (2:12-14). Commentators agree that all of these assurances apply to all Christians. However, John is emphasizing for each group of Christians the particular assurances that are most important for that group.

Some people think "dear children" refers to all of John's readers, as it does in 2:1,28. In that case, John is dividing all Christians into two groups—mature (fathers) and less mature (young men). Other people think John has three groups in mind: newborn Christians, spiritual warriors, and mature elders.

Name (2:12). In Scripture, a person's name often symbolizes his character (Psalm 44:5, Acts 3:16). We are forgiven on account of the merits and character of Jesus, not on our own merits.

2. Choose one of the assurances in 2:12-14 and explain why it is especially encouraging to you.

_____

_____

_____

_____

_____

_____

The world (2:15-17)

World (2:15). *Kosmos* is a key word in John's writings. Its root meaning is "ornament" (as in 1 Peter 3:3), and it gives us our word "cosmetic." It also has the sense of "order," the opposite of chaos. From there it came to be used for the universe, the greatest ordered ornament. The most important part of the universe for humans is this earth, so it, too, came to be called "the world." It was natural, then, to think of the world as the majority of people. In particular the human world order—social, economic, political, and religious systems—was called the *kosmos*. But the majority of people have always been caught up in their world systems and resistant to God. They rejected and finally crucified Christ. So, John and the other New Testament writers often use *kosmos* to name the world of those "hostile to Christ and all that He stands for."[1] In this sense, the world is corrupted by sin, so it is evil, dangerous, futile, temporary. Satan dominates the world (John 12:31, 1 John 5:19), that is, the world of people who are not yet born of God and freed from darkness. The world of sinful men has become an evil world system controlled by the evil one. That which God created to be a lovely and ordered ornament became an ugly and strife-torn world order because men rejected God and fell under the control of evil. This is the sense of "world" in 1 John 2:15-17.

However, God loves the world of men and sent His Son to save it (John 3:16, 4:42, 6:51; 1 John 2:2, 4:14). The world of men is dominated by the wicked order and those who control it, but God means to rescue the world (of helpless people) from the world (enslaved by Satan's system and men's own wickedness).

Thus, "world" has many shades of meaning, and John shifts from one to another without warning or uses the word in several senses at once. When you see it in a given passage, think carefully about what it means there.

Love of the Father (2:15). As in 2:5, this could be the Father's love for us. However, the context suggests that it is our love for the Father.

3. Recall what "love" means (pages 52-53). In what sense should Christians love the world (1 John 4:14)? (*Optional:* See John 3:16, 2 Corinthians 5:18-20.)

_____

_____

_____

For Further Study: Look up *world* in a concordance (see page 144). Study all the references in John's Gospel and epistles. (What is the world? How does God feel about it? How should Christians treat the world?) Then, if you like, study references to the world in Paul's epistles and in the other New Testament books.

**For Thought and
Discussion:** In what
areas have you been
freed from loving the
world?

_____

_____

_____

4. However, in what sense should we not love the
   world (1 John 2:15-17)?

_____

_____

_____

_____

_____

5. Why can't we love both the world and the
   Father (2:15)? (*Optional:* See Luke 16:13,
   1 John 2:16.)

_____

_____

_____

_____

_____

_____

Cravings of sinful man (2:16). "Lust of the flesh" in
KJV. "The flesh" is not the physical body, but
rather man's lower, corrupt nature. "The lust[s]
of the flesh" are godless desires, especially sen-
sual ones: gluttony, moral laxity, love of pleas-
ure and luxury, stinginess, materialism, and so
on.[2]

Lust of his eyes (2:16). Primarily covetousness of
what one sees and concern for appearances. The
desire to "keep up with the Joneses"[3] regarding
the appearance of one's home, car, and other
possessions, one's job status and social posi-
tion, one's children's reputation in school, etc.

To crave a glamorous, sophisticated, or successful image is also to lust in this way.

Boasting of what he has and does (2:16). "Pride of life" in KJV. "Pride that glories not so much in doing well as in being better than one's fellows."[4] A need to prove that one is superior in achievement, intellect, possessions, beauty, talent, etc.—exalting oneself at others' expense. The pride of life is also the belief that one can succeed on one's own strength, without God's help.

Optional Application: Do you use the world's means to control others and serve yourself in any ways? Talk with God about this.

6. Do you struggle against any of the temptations John lists in 2:16? If so, give one example of each that you face.

cravings of sinful man _____

_____

_____

_____

lust of his eyes _____

_____

_____

_____

boasting of what he has and does _____

_____

_____

_____

7. Why is it foolish to love the world rather than the Father (2:17)?

_____

_____

_____

_____

For Further Study:
a. Compare 1 John
2:15-16 to Romans
8:5-8. How does each
passage illuminate
the other?
    b. According to
Romans 8:5-13, how
can a person resist
the love of the sinful
world system?

_____

_____

8. Is there any insight from 2:12-17 that you
   would like to concentrate on for growth this
   week? If so, what is it?

_____

_____

_____

_____

_____

9. How do you observe this truth already at work
   in your life?

_____

_____

_____

_____

_____

10. How would you like it to change your life?

_____

_____

_____

_____

_____

_____

11. What can you do to cooperate with God in apply-
    ing this truth?

_____

_____

_____
_____
_____

Study Skill—Obstacles to Application

Here are some of the most frequent obstacles to applying God's Word:

1. "I didn't have time to meditate on and pray about a passage this week." What do you think about while in the car, getting dressed, or doing other things besides working and talking? Most people have at least a few minutes a day in which they can think about God rather than earthly concerns. Try turning off the radio and television, and just be quiet with God.

2. "I pray, study, and meditate every morning, but I forget to think about Scripture during my free moments." Make reminders: tape a card with a reminder or quotation to your dashboard, refrigerator, desk, or mirror. Tie a string on your finger, purse, or briefcase. Try any gimmick that helps! It's important to let biblical teaching come to mind frequently during the day so that it will begin to affect your automatic responses to sudden situations.

3. "I can't ever think of specific ways to act on what the Scripture says." One key is prayer. Choose a passage, and each day pray about it, asking God to teach you what it means and to lead you into ways of applying it. If you like, divide your life into spheres (home, work, church, school . . .) or people (spouse, children, parents, co-workers, church friends . . .). Choose one person, and pray about what that person needs from you, what might prevent you from fulfilling that need, and how you might fulfill that need. Or, review a recent situation in which you sinned. Look for a similar situation in the near future to act rightly. Ask God to enable you to recognize and respond rightly to the situation.

Persistent prayer, in which you invite God to show you opportunities to apply what you have learned, will be answered.

Optional Application: Does 2:16 suggest any specific temptation you are fighting to resist by God's grace? If so, confess it to God, thank Him for what John wrote in 2:13 about the children and in 2:14 about the young men, and ask God for strength to resist the love of the world.

For Further Study: If you are making an outline of 1 John, add 2:12-17 to it.

12. List any questions you have about 2:12-17.

_____

_____

_____

_____

For the group

Warm-up. Ask, "What part of your life are you most
proud of?" This could be a talent like intellect, effi-
ciency, musical accomplishment, or athletic ability.
It could be an attribute like good looks or a posses-
sion like fine clothes or high tech equipment. It
could be a virtue like politeness, hospitality, or
generosity. Encourage everyone to be honest with
himself or herself, even if he or she doesn't want to
tell the group. Even good things like hospitality or
neutral things like intellect can feed worldliness if we
exalt them as part of our precious self-image. This
brief examination of your hearts should be a good
preparation for discussing lust and pride, as well as
forgiveness and overcoming. You might plan to pray
about your areas of pride after your discussion.

Read aloud and summarize.

Questions. In lesson four you confessed your disobedience and lack of love, and you committed
yourselves to changing by God's grace. This lesson
illuminates some of the things that keep us from
love and obedience: lust and pride. Once you understand what 2:12-17 says, apply it to some of your
cravings and objects of pride (such as those you
thought of in the warm-up). Why do you need to
turn from those things, according to 2:15-17? What
motivations for repentance does 2:12-14 offer? How
is it possible for you to overcome worldliness,
according to 2:12-17? Does anyone in the group
know other scriptures that suggest ways of overcoming sin? When you have discussed enough, let each
person commit him or herself to repenting of one
aspect of worldliness (or to some other application).
Then pray for each other.

Worship. Thank God that your sins have been forgiven, that you know the Father and Jesus who are from the beginning, and that you have overcome the evil one because the Word of God lives in you. Thank God for the power to overcome the lusts and pride of the world that tempt each of you.

1. Burdick, pages 176-177; Leon Morris, *The Gospel According to John* (Grand Rapids, Michigan: William B. Eerdmans Publishing Company, 1971), page 127.
2. Boice, pages 78-79; Burdick, page 179.
3. Boice, page 79.
4. Boice, page 79.

1 JOHN 2:18-28, 4:1-6

The Test of Truth

"Who is the liar? It is the man who denies that Jesus is the Christ."
                    1 John 2:22

John has indicted the false teachers for being indifferent to righteousness and love, but he is not finished. Plenty of people in the world claim to please God by pursuing justice and love, but that is not good enough. There is one more crucial proof that a person really has fellowship with God.
       Read 2:18-28 and 4:1-6.

The Father and the Son (2:18-28)

1. John talks about *truth* repeatedly in 2:18-28. Why? What is the passage about?

_____

_____

_____

_____

_____

The last hour (2:18). Jewish teaching discerned two ages—"this age" and "the age to come" (the

69

For Further Study:
Study the meaning of
anointing in the Old
Testament. See, for
example, Exodus
29:1-9, 1 Samuel
10:1, and 2 Kings
11:12.

**For Thought and
Discussion:** In 2:19,
John criticizes those
who "went out from
us." In your judgment,
does his criticism
apply to people who
move to different
churches? To those
who change denomi-
nations? To those
who start new denom-
inations? To those
who leave Christianity
entirely? By what
standards do we
decide whether
someone has gone
"out from us"? (See,
for example, Luke
9:49-50, 11:23;
1 Corinthians 5:9-13.)

Kingdom of God, the Messianic Age). The end
of the first and the beginning of the second
would be heralded by "the last days" and finally
"the day of the Lord."

The New Testament teaches that the last
days began when Jesus came to earth (Acts
2:17, Hebrews 1:2, 1 Peter 1:20). The Incarnation, and especially the Crucifixion and Resurrection, marked the beginning of the end for
this age. The age to come has started for those
who are in Christ and therefore in the Kingdom
of God, but the age to come will not be fully
here until Christ returns. Since there is no age
between this age and the age to come, all the
time between Christ's first and second comings
is the last days, the end times, the last hour.
How long the last hour will go on until *the* last
hour, nobody but God knows.

Antichrist(s) (2:18). This word occurs only in John's
letters (1 John 2:18,22; 4:3; 2 John 7), but the
idea recurs throughout the New Testament.
John mentions it as though it is familiar to his
readers.

At the end of this age, the Jews expected
that there would be a great battle between the
forces of good led by God and the forces of evil
led by a cunning, powerful, and wicked being.
Daniel foresaw him as a "beast" (Daniel 7:7-27),
as did John (Revelation 13:1-18). Paul called
him "the man of lawlessness" (2 Thessalonians
2:3). Jesus promised "false Christs and false
prophets" (Mark 13:22). John's readers knew
him as "the antichrist" which means "opposite
of Christ" or "instead of Christ." That is, he is
either the utter opposite of Christ because of his
wickedness and his efforts to thwart salvation,
or he is someone claiming to be Christ the Savior of the world. He may be both.

John does not deny the fact that *the*
antichrist will come, but he says that fore-
runners of that one, sharing his character,
spirit, and aims, have already come. These will
be present as long as the last hour lasts.

Anointing (2:20). The Greek word is *chrisma,* from
which we get the English word *chrism,* "anointing oil." Just as Jesus was shown to be the

Christ (the Anointed One) when the Holy Spirit came upon Him at His baptism, so we become "anointed ones" when God anoints us with the Holy Spirit. The chrism of the Holy Spirit protects us from the wiles of the antichrists, who are anointed with a different spirit.[1]

Know (2:20). The Gnostics claimed to know certain truths necessary for salvation that the other Christians did not know. John insists that the anointing and the apostles' teaching have imparted all that his readers need to know to be saved. They require no Gnostic teaching (2:26-27).

For Thought and Discussion: a. How does the inner anointing of the Holy Spirit teach us (2:27)? (Is it something we can feel or measure?)

b. Why do we need *both* the inner anointing and the factual information of the Bible for proper teaching? What role does each one play in training us?

For Thought and Discussion: Why is it crucial that Jesus is fully man and fully God?

2. How can we recognize a false teacher, someone influenced by the spirit of antichrist?

2:19 _____

_____

_____

_____

2:22-23 _____

_____

_____

3. Two things protect John's readers (and us) from being swayed by the antichrists. What are our guides and guardians?

2:20,27 _____

2:24 _____

4. If we "all . . . know the truth" (2:20) and "do not need anyone to teach" us (2:27) because of our anointing, does this mean that we don't need preachers and Bible teachers? Why or why not? (*Optional:* See Ephesians 4:11-13.)

_____

_____

71

For Thought and Discussion: Explain in your own words what God sent Jesus to be and do (2:1-2; 4:9-10,14-15).

For Thought and Discussion: John uses the word "remain" (abide, continue) six times in 2:18-28. What does he say about remaining?

Jesus is the Christ (2:22). "The man Jesus is the divine Christ."[2] _Christ_ is the Greek translation of the Hebrew _Messiah_, which means "Anointed One." The Jews believed that this was simply a human king. However, when Greeks heard Christians calling Jesus "the Christ" and "the Son of God," they knew nothing about the Jewish idea. They thought of the Christ as a divine being, a savior, an emissary from God. The Gnostics taught that the Christ descended upon Jesus at his baptism and left him before his crucifixion, so Jesus was not himself the Christ. (See page 12.) But John insists that Jesus is the Christ and the Son of God, fully divine. The Son of God has come "in the flesh" (4:2); that is, He who "was from the beginning" (1:1) became fully human.

5. John says it is impossible to "have" or "know" the Father if we disbelieve in the Son (2:23). Why is this so? (See 1 John 2:1-2; 4:9-10,14-15; 5:11-12. _Optional:_ See John 1:18, 8:19, 12:44, 14:7-9, 15:23.)

_____

_____

_____

_____

_____

_____

_____

_____

Remain(s) (2:24). This word implies permanence: "remain," "abide," "stay," "dwell," "endure." In particular, John likes to use it to express the permanent relationship among the Father, the Son, and the believer (John 15:4-10).[3]

In the Son and in the Father (2:24). In intimate fellowship and union with them.

6. John says that if our anointing and what we have heard *remain in us*, then we will *remain in the Son and in the Father* (2:24). Why is it so important to remain in them? (*Optional:* See John 15:1-8, Romans 6:3-10, 1 John 2:28.)

_____

_____

_____

_____

_____

_____

_____

For Further Study: Compare John's test in 1 John 4:1-3 to the Old Testament test for prophets in Deuteronomy 13:1-5, 18:14-22. What do the two have in common?

For Thought and Discussion: Do *we* need to test the spiritual origins of prophesies and teachings, as well as whether or not they are true? Why or why not?

The Spirit and the Son (4:1-6)

In chapter 3, John returns to discuss the ethical tests—righteousness and love—on a deeper level than in chapter 2, and he begins to weave them together. Then, in 3:24 he makes his first explicit reference to the Holy Spirit (although 2:20 alluded to Him). This leads John back to the test of truth: it helps us discern not only who knows the Father, but also who is inspired by the Spirit. The Gnostic troublemakers were not just teachers who claimed to know the Father; they were also prophets who claimed to speak by the direct inspiration of the Holy Spirit. Since the early Church recognized that some Christians were prophets (Acts 11:27-30; 1 Corinthians 14:1-5,22-33), John needed to help his flock discern true prophets from false ones.

For Thought and Discussion: Why is it impossible for a religious or philosophical teacher to be inspired neither by the Holy Spirit nor by the spirit of antichrist?

For Thought and Discussion: In what sense have John's readers "overcome" the false teachers (4:4)?

For Thought and Discussion: According to 4:5, why are false teachers so often popular?

Acknowledges (4:2). "Confesses" in RSV. This is not just intellectual knowledge, for even the demons agree that Jesus is the Son of God, and they shudder (Mark 1:24, James 2:19). Instead, this is an open and bold profession that Jesus is the incarnate Lord, God, and Savior.[4]

You . . . They . . . We (4:4-6). These words are emphatic in the Greek; John is contrasting who is and isn't from God.[5]

7. Why isn't it arrogant for John to say "whoever knows God listens to us; but whoever is not from God does not listen to us" (4:6)? Recall 1:1-4.

_____

_____

_____

_____

_____

8. Is the test in 4:1-3 useful to you in any ways? If so, how? If not, why not?

_____

_____

_____

_____

_____

_____

9. How can 4:4 be an encouragement to you as you deal with false teaching or other temptation?

_____

_____

_____

_____

_____

_____

10. Reread 2:18-28 and 4:1-6, and summarize each
    passage in a sentence or two.

    2:18-28 _____

    _____

    _____

    _____

    4:1-6 _____

    _____

    _____

    _____

    _____

11. What have you found in 2:18-28 or 4:1-6 that
    you would like to concentrate on for application
    during the next week?

    _____

    _____

    _____

    _____

12. How is this truth already affecting your life?

    _____

    _____

    _____

    _____

For Thought and Discussion: a. Are there any groups teaching Gnostic-like doctrines in our day? If so, who are they, and how can you identify them?

b. What should Christians do and not do about such groups?

Optional Application: Pray for any people you know who are tempted to follow the teaching and behavior of groups who deny that Jesus is the one and only Christ.

Optional Application: Meditate this week on the fact that Jesus is the Christ. What does this mean, and what implications does it have for your life? (See questions 5 and 6. You might focus on one of the passages in question 5.)

Optional Application: Pray about the fact that the One who is in you is greater than the one who is in the world (4:4). How should this fact affect how you think and what you do this week?

For Further Study: If you are making an outline of 1 John, you can add 2:18-28 to it.

13. How do you fall short or want to grow in this area?

_____

_____

_____

_____

_____

14. What can you do this week to cooperate with God in achieving this growth?

_____

_____

_____

_____

_____

_____

15. List any questions you have about 2:18-28 or 4:1-6.

_____

_____

_____

_____

For the group

Warm-up. How has believing that Jesus is the Christ affected what you have done this week?

Questions. Try not to get drawn into a discussion of the end times and the antichrist, since this is not what John is teaching about in this letter. Make sure everyone understands what "the last hour," "the antichrist," and "antichrists" mean, and then move to studying 2:18-28 and 4:1-6 themselves.

John has a harsh, absolute attitude toward the false teachers whom he saw as wolves bloodying his sheep. Discuss how you should think about and treat groups who teach that Jesus is not the Christ in the sense that John means it. If you have encountered real instances of false teaching, consider what leaders and members of churches and fellowships should do when they discern falsehood in someone in their midst. Also, examine your own hearts: do you think and act as though you fully believe that Jesus is the Christ? How can your actions better reflect this belief? Without mentioning names in the group, you might pray for people you know who are attracted to doctrines that deny Christ.

Worship. Thank God for the inner anointing and the apostles' teaching that He has given to you. Thank Him for having all antichrists well under control. Praise Jesus as the fully human man who was and is the eternal Son of God. Thank Him for coming in the flesh and giving His life for you. Thank Him for leading you to have fellowship with the Father.

1. Stott, pages 106, 109-110.
2. *The NIV Study Bible,* edited by Kenneth Barker (Grand Rapids, Michigan: Zondervan Corporation, 1985), page 1910.
3. Raymond E. Brown, *The Gospel According to John (I-XII),* volume 29 (Garden City: Doubleday and Company, 1966), page 510.
4. Stott, page 154.
5. Stott, pages 156-158.

1 JOHN 2:29-3:10

Children of God

"This is how we know who the children of God are and who the children of the devil are: Anyone who does not do what is right is not a child of God. . . ."
1 John 3:10a

John has been explaining how we may know that we have fellowship with God (1:6)—that we know God (2:3) and dwell with God (2:24). He has given us two kinds of tests: ethical (obedience, love) and doctrinal (belief in Jesus). Now, as he goes back to develop these tests further, he shows us our relationship with God on a deeper level. We not only have fellowship with God, but we are also His children (2:29-3:10)!

In the discourse on fellowship (1:5-2:28), John described the ethical test as walking in the light. This included obeying God, confessing our sins when we disobey, and loving our brothers (1:5-2:11). In this second discourse on the new birth (2:29-4:6), John speaks only of obedience and love, elaborating them and weaving them together.

As you read 2:29-3:10, sense how John feels about rebirth and righteousness.

Children (3:1). When Paul calls us "sons" of God in Romans 8:14,23, he uses a Greek word (*uios*) that describes a legal relationship. Even an adopted child is a "son" in this sense and inherits his father's outward possessions. But in

For Thought and Discussion: In what ways will we be like Christ when He returns? (See Ephesians 4:24, Philippians 3:21.)

For Thought and Discussion: Why should we want to be like Christ (3:2)?

Optional Application: Is your hope fully fixed on being like Jesus when He appears? Do your actions show it? How can you more fully set your hope on Jesus?

1 John 3:1,7,10, John uses a word for "children" (*teknia*) that stresses the natural genetic relationship, not the legal one.[1] An adopted child cannot be a *teknon*. John declares that we have been "born of God" (2:29, 3:9). God's seed (*sperma*) resides in us (3:9), and it is the seed of a father that carries "the life principle as well as the hereditary characteristics."[2] The spiritual genetic material of God is at work in anyone born of God, guaranteeing that the child will grow up displaying the Father's features.

1. How does John feel about being a child of God? How does he express his feelings in 3:1?

_____

_____

_____

_____

_____

_____

He . . . him (3:2-3). John often calls both the Father and Christ "he" without telling which he means. In 3:2 it is Christ who will appear. Christ is also the one called "pure" in 3:3.

2. We don't yet understand what the full, final results of our rebirth will be, but we do know something about them. What will be the ultimate effect of God's seed in us (3:2)?

_____

_____

_____

_____

_____

3. What do you think it will mean to be like Christ? (*Optional:* See 1 Corinthians 15:42-49, Ephesians 4:24, Philippians 3:21.)

_____

_____

_____

_____

_____

4. Why does a child of God do what is right and constantly purify himself from sin (2:29; 3:2-3,9)?

_____

_____

_____

_____

_____

For Thought and Discussion: a. Why does the hope of 3:2 motivate us to purify ourselves?

b. What has Jesus done that enables us to purify ourselves from sin? Why is this crucial to remember? What happens when we forget this?

For Thought and Discussion: a. Why is "lawlessness" especially inconceivable for a child of God?

b. What does 3:4 imply about a sinner's attitude toward God?

Optional Application: Is there any lawlessness left in your heart? If so, what should you do about it?

Hope (3:3). Not a wish, but something you expect with certainty.

Sin is lawlessness (3:4). "Sin" means literally, "missing the mark" and could refer to any flaw, weakness, or failure to live up to God's standards. "Lawlessness" refers to deliberate rebellion against God's will.[3]

Take away our sins (3:5). By speaking of "sins" in the plural, John seems to mean not that Christ came to bear the guilt and penalty of our sin (which is true), but that He came to remove our sinful practices. This fact justifies John's claim in 3:6.[4]

Jesus has finished taking away our sins in a legal sense (Hebrews 10:11-18), but He has not yet finished taking away our sinful habits and practices.

81

For Thought and Discussion: How has Jesus already destroyed the devil's work? How is He still destroying it? What work is He destroying?

For Thought and Discussion: Why aren't 1:8 and 3:9 contradictory?

For Thought and Discussion: Although we have been justified by grace apart from works (Ephesians 2:8), why can't we be unconcerned about how righteous our behavior is?

Optional Application: Are you ever tempted to be lax about your conduct because you know you are saved by grace? Pray about this.

5. Sin is inconsistent with *the Father's nature* (1:5, 2:29), so it is inconsistent for His children as well. It is also inconsistent with *Christ's nature* (3:3,5), and we are becoming like the Son of God (3:2-3).

How is sin also incompatible with *Christ's work on earth* (3:5,8)?

_____

_____

_____

_____

_____

_____

6. The *source of sin* is another reason why it is inconceivable for a reborn person to practice sin. What is the source of sin, and why does this make sin and rebirth incompatible (3:8,10)?

_____

_____

_____

_____

_____

Keeps on sinning . . . continues to sin (3:6,9). These verses have perplexed Christians for centuries. They state that believers do not and cannot sin, while almost all Christians are acutely aware that they do sin. Here are some of the explanations that have been offered:

1. By "sin," John means only "notorious crimes, or offenses against love."[5] (However, John gives no indication that he means this, and Christians sometimes do commit adultery, theft, and even murder.)

2. "The Christian 'cannot' sin because what is sin in the life of an unbeliever is not so

82

regarded by God in a believer."[6] (This sounds like the kind of perverse claim John's opponents would make. John himself says "Everyone who sins breaks the law . . ." [3:4]).

3. The old nature in a person continues to sin, but the new nature cannot sin. (The false teachers would like this doctrine also, for it allows a person to deny guilt for his misdeeds. "It wasn't the real me, so I'm not responsible," he might argue. According to Scripture, a person's two natures may war within him for control, but it is always the person who yields to one of his natures and so sins or resists.[7])

4. John is describing not present reality, but the ideal to which Christians should aspire. Theoretically, Christians cannot sin, although in fact most of us do. (Does 3:4-10 sound like an assertion of facts or ideals? Is lofty idealism a good way to refute false teachers?)

5. Christians cannot sin willfully; they only fall into sin against their wills. (However, just as David seduced Bathsheba while knowing it was wrong, so most Christians can think of times when they have deliberately disobeyed God.)

6. John is talking about the "spiritually elite,"[8] the saints who no longer sin. (But are only the elite born of God? Can there be a saved Christian who is not born of God? See John 3:3.)

7. John means that in so far as a person is abiding in Christ, to that extent he cannot sin.[9] (This makes sense of 3:6, but what about 3:9? In that verse, either one is born of God—and does not sin—or one is not born of God—and does sin. There is no "in so far as.")

8. "John refers to the eschatological reality brought about by Christ's coming, namely the possibility that is open to believers, which is both a fact ('he cannot sin') and conditional (if he lives in him')."[10] (But isn't "he is able not to sin" different from "he is not able to sin"?)

9. The Greek present tense describes a continuous process in the present. The aorist tense denotes individual actions in the present. John uses the present tense in 3:6,9. Therefore, the NIV translates "keeps on sinning," "continues to sin," and "go on sinning." John

Optional Application: If 2:29-3:10 gives you reason to doubt that you are a child of God, confess your sins and ask God to give you that new birth if you lack it. Discuss your situation with a mature Christian to discern whether your rebelliousness shows that you are not saved or just reveals areas in which you still need to grow. Ask that person to pray with you to abandon sin. Let 1:8-2:2 keep you from despair and 3:1-3 motivate you to change. You might also pray about Ephesians 3:16-21 and Philippians 2:12-13.

For Thought and Discussion: a. Can a person with a persistent, compulsive sin (such as alcoholism, pride, gossip, lust) be a Christian if he persistently confesses his sin, yet continues in it? Explain your reasoning.

b. What about if he does not frequently confess?

For Thought and Discussion: What should a church or fellowship do if a member is practicing sin? (See Matthew 18:15-20, 1 Corinthians 5:1-13, 2 Corinthians 2:5-11.)

knows that God's children will commit individual acts of sin that require confession, repentance, and forgiveness (1:8-10). But they cannot persist unrepentant in habitual sin. This kind of willful disregard for God's laws (lawlessness) is evidence that someone has not been reborn.[11] (However, some New Testament scholars dispute this view of Greek tenses.[12])

In choosing among these interpretations, remember that 3:6,9 is a test we can apply by observing what people *do*. It is a standard by which we can tell true teachers from false ones and by which we can be sure we are born of God. Somehow, we are able to observe people's lives and discern fairly accurately whether they are God's children (Matthew 7:15-23).

7. What do you think it means to say that a child of God cannot sin (3:9)?

_____

_____

_____

_____

_____

8. Examine your own life in light of 2:29-3:10. To what extent do you act like a child of God, and to what extent do you act like a child of the devil? Spend some time in confession, if necessary. From what habits do you need to purify yourself (3:3)?

_____

_____

_____

_____

_____

_____

84

9. How can you actively do what is right and/or purify yourself this week? Think of some specific actions and matters for prayer.

_____

_____

_____

_____

_____

_____

10. Summarize what you've learned from 2:29-3:10.

_____

_____

_____

_____

11. List any questions you still have about this passage.

_____

_____

_____

_____

For Thought and Discussion: Does John imply that we can attain perfect purity in this life (3:2-3)? Explain, drawing on other parts of his letter, if necessary.

For Thought and Discussion: Is righteous behavior a *condition* of being born of God or an *evidence* of it? How do you know? Why is the distinction important?

For Further Study: Add 2:29-3:10 to your outline of 1 John.

For the group

Warm-up. Take a few minutes to review how everyone's applications from the last few weeks are progressing. Encourage and help each other when possible.

Read aloud and summarize.

Questions. Ask what it means to be a child of God. Have someone explain why John is so excited about being one (3:1). Then get the group to list and explain all the reasons why Christians should not and cannot practice sin. Do wrestle some with the meaning of 3:6,9, but be prepared for uncertainty and disagreement. Fine Bible students have struggled with these verses for centuries.

Once you understand the passage fairly well, focus on questions 8 and 9. You should know and trust each other well enough by now to share some of your real struggles. Pray for repentance and the grace to change.

Worship. Thank God for making you His children who have inherited and are increasingly showing His characteristics. Thank Christ for taking away your sins and destroying the devil's work. Praise the Father and Christ for being righteous, pure, and without sin. Thank God for the hope that you will be like Christ in His character as well as in His eternal life. Pray for help to purify yourselves and do what is right.

1. Burdick, page 230.
2. Burdick, page 247; compare Stott, pages 129-130.
3. Burdick, pages 236-237.
4. Burdick, pages 237-238.
5. Stott, page 131. Augustine, Bede, and Luther held this view.
6. Stott, page 131.
7. Stott, pages 131-132.
8. Burdick, page 244.
9. John F. Walvoord and Roy Zuck, *The Bible Knowledge Commentary* (Wheaton, Illinois: Victor Books/Scripture Press, 1983), page 895.
10. I. Howard Marshall, *The Epistles of John* (Grand Rapids, Michigan: William B. Eerdmans Publishing Company, 1978), pages 182-183.
11. Burdick, page 246; Stott, page 135.
12. Marshall, page 180, note 8.

1 JOHN 3:11-24

Love in Action

"We know that we have passed from death to life, because we love our brothers. Anyone who does not love remains in death."
                    1 John 3:14

In 2:7-11 John said love demonstrates that we walk in the light and even helps us to do so. Now he explores more fully the meaning and the fruits of love. Read 3:10-24 to see the connection between this passage and 2:29-3:10. You might also want to review the definition of love on pages 52-53.

The love test (3:11-15)

Cain (3:12). He was the first murderer. He killed his brother Abel because God rejected Cain's sacrifice and accepted Abel's (Genesis 4:1-16).

From death to life (3:14). Without rebirth into God's family, a person is spiritually dead (Ephesians 2:1-5). Rebirth is not a question of passing from one kind of spiritual life to another.

Brothers (3:14). When Jesus discussed the Old Testament command, "Love your neighbor as yourself," He explained that a neighbor was any person, not just a member of one's own community (Leviticus 19:18, Luke 10:25-37). But His "new command" for His disciples was, "Love each

Optional Application: Do the ways you treat certain other believers reveal any areas of hate in you? Is there anyone you are refusing to love? If so, how does this affect your relationship with God? What can you do about this?

other as I have loved you" (John 13:34, 15:12-13). The "each other" in John 13:34 and the "brothers" in 1 John 3:14 are fellow Christians, not mankind in general. The test of being God's child is whether we love our fellow Christians. This doesn't mean that loving nonChristians is unimportant—Jesus commands it. But love for God's children is one of the acid tests of whether a person is born of God. Why? Because "everyone who loves the father [God] loves his child [believers, those who are born of God] as well" (1 John 5:1). Loving the family members is one of the proofs that we are part of the family. Even false teachers might claim that they love their neighbors, but their hatred for God's children proves they are not part of His family. Our family love shouldn't be bigoted favoritism, but it should be a priority in our lives.[1]

1. What do we know is true of us if we . . .

   love our fellow believers (3:14)? _____

   _____

   _____

   hate our fellow believers (3:14-15)? _____

   _____

   _____

   _____

2. The absence of love is hate (2:9-11), and to hate is to be a murderer (3:12,15). Why is refusal to love the same as murder? (What do the two have in common?)

   _____

   _____

   _____

   _____

   _____

3. Cain killed his brother because of his brother's righteousness (3:12). Why do the wicked hate the righteous so much that they may even desire their death?

_____

_____

_____

_____

_____

4. Why shouldn't Christians be surprised if the world hates them (3:13)?

_____

_____

_____

_____

The test of love (3:16-18)

5. Love for other Christians proves that we have eternal life (3:14-15). But how can we discern genuine from fake love? Explain all the standards for identifying love you find in 3:16-18.

3:16 _____

_____

_____

3:17 _____

_____

3:18 _____

_____

_____

For Further Study:
On 3:13, see Luke
6:22-23.

**For Thought and
Discussion:** How can
we tell if we are being
persecuted for right-
eousness or for some
other reason?

**For Thought and
Discussion:** Why is
Godlike love so diffi-
cult for most of us to
exhibit? What beliefs,
priorities, fears, etc.
make us more prone
to hatred than love?

For Further Study:
a. For more on Jesus'
example of love
(3:16), see Philippi-
ans 2:5-11.
    b. For ways in
which we can do
likewise, see Philip-
pians 2:1-4.

6. Why is it so crucial to meet people's material
   needs, not just to pray for, talk to, or witness to
   them (3:17)?

_____

_____

_____

_____

_____

7. How could you love someone this week according to the definition in 3:16-18? (Talk with God
   about this, and try to come up with some specific ideas.)

_____

_____

_____

_____

_____

_____

The love of God (3:17). Not our love for God, but
    God's *agape* dwelling in and flowing through
    us. If God's active, selfless love isn't flowing
    through us to other believers, then we may
    doubt that He is in us at all.[2]

Dealing with doubt (3:19-24)

God is greater than our hearts (3:20). God's greater
    knowledge could be a reason for fear, since if
    our hearts condemn us, how much worse could
    God's perfect knowledge condemn us! In this
    case, John is showing why we desperately need
    an assurance of our salvation to *set our hearts
    at rest* (3:19).

On the other hand, God's greater knowledge could be part of the assurance. God knows even the tiniest sprout of love from His seed within us. While the absence of impressive fruit may trouble our hearts, we may take comfort from the fact that God sees our smallest beginnings and judges more accurately than we do.

Confidence (3:21). This was a high privilege in the Greek world. It originally meant the right of a full citizen of a democracy to speak in the citizens' assembly. Later it came to mean freedom to speak with frankness and courage. Thus, in 2:28 and 3:21, confidence is the right to speak frankly and boldly to Christ at His second coming and to God even now in prayer.[3]

8. How do we know we "belong to the truth" (3:19)? And how do we "set our hearts at rest in his presence" (3:19)? See 3:18-20.

_____

_____

_____

_____

_____

9. If our hearts do not condemn us because the test in 3:18-20 sets them at rest, what are the results (3:21)?

_____

_____

_____

_____

_____

10. What are some of the conditions we must meet in order to obtain this promise (3:22-23)?

_____

Optional Application: Are there any believers with material needs in your community? How can you help see that those people are aided?

For Thought and Discussion: a. Why do you think John focuses on love for believers in 3:11-24, rather than including all people?

b. According to John 13:35 and 17:21-23, why is it important that we love other Christians?

For Thought and Discussion: If you think a brother's material needs are due to irresponsibility, what should you do? (Consider 2 Thessalonians 3:6-15.)

Optional Application: Measure yourself by 3:16-18. Does your heart condemn you, or do you have confidence? Ask God to give you discernment in this area.

For Further Study:
Compare 1 John 3:23
to Matthew 22:34-40.
How are Jesus' and
John's versions of
God's commands
related? (See also
Jesus' version in John
13:34, 15:12-13.)

For Further Study:
a. For other conditions
of answered prayer
besides 1 John
3:22-23, see Psalm
66:18, Matthew
21:22, Mark 11:25,
John 16:23-24, and
James 4:2-3.
     b. If our prayers
are not answered,
does that mean we
are in sin? Why or
why not?

**For Thought and
Discussion:** a. How
does God's Spirit
assure us that God
lives in us and we in
Him (3:24)? See
Romans 8:16.
     b. Is this a new,
almost mystical basis
for confidence in
addition to faith, love,
and obedience? Or is
the Spirit somehow
related to these
three? (See Galatians
5:16,22-23.)

11. What one insight from 3:11-24 seems most sig-
    nificant to you?

12. How do you observe this already at work in your
    life?

13. Is there any way you would like to respond to
    this truth, other than what you wrote in ques-
    tion 7? If so, what do you plan to do? (This
    could include memorizing, meditating, praying,
    and doing what John says.)

14. List any questions you have about 3:11-24.

For the group

Warm-up. Ask each person to share one act of love or hate that he or she has experienced recently. When you've examined John's definitions of love and hate, come back to these experiences and see if they fit the definitions. You can just ask for experiences of love if you feel that focusing on being treated with hate encourages people to feel angry or depressed.

Application. John's words are meant to reassure believers, not make us feel condemned. If you feel you do not live up to his test of love, ask God for forgiveness and the grace to change (remember 1:8-10). Look for specific ways of actively loving people you know. There may be needy believers in your church or community whom you could actively love together. Or, you may be able to support each others' efforts in prayer during your meeting and throughout the coming week.

Worship. Praise God for being greater than your hearts when they condemn you. Thank Him for putting His Spirit within you to guarantee that God lives in you and you in Him. Thank God for giving you assurance that you have passed from death to life. Thank Jesus for laying down His life for you, thus revealing how you should act. Thank Father, Son, and Spirit for showing you how you should live and for providing the grace to do so.

1. Burdick, pages 145-146, 265.
2. Burdick, page 270.
3. Burdick, pages 208-209, 276.

For Thought and Discussion: In 3:10,22-23 John interweaves the tests of knowing God (obedience, love, and faith). How are the three related, according to these verses?

Optional Application: Does 3:22 help to explain why your prayers are not always answered? If so, confess and repent of ways in which you act with hatred or disobedience. Ask God to help you see and do what pleases Him.

For Further Study: Add 3:11-24 to your outline.

1 JOHN 4:7-5:1

God Is Love

"Whoever does not love does not know God, because God is love."
                          1 John 4:8

John began to weave the tests of assurance together in 3:10,23—faith and love together are obedience and demonstrate who are the children of God. Now John unfolds the deepest connection between the truth about Christ and the obligation to love, a connection that flows from the very nature of God Himself.

Reread John's definition of love in 3:16-18 along with 4:7-5:1.

Love comes from God (4:7). Literally, "the *agape* is from God." Sexual passion, parental devotion, and friendly affection are not necessarily totally from God. All three can be tainted with selfishness and based on the beloved's worthiness. Only *agape*—a selfless commitment to do good to someone regardless of whether he deserves it—comes completely from God and is part of His essential nature.

1. Why did God send His Son into the world?

   4:9 _____

For Further Study:
a. Compare 1 John 4:8 to John 4:24, Hebrews 12:29, and 1 John 1:5. What do we know about God's essential nature?
   b. Why is it important to remember that God is *both* light (truth, holiness) and love?

For Thought and Discussion: What does it mean to say that God is love?

95

Optional Application: a. Apply John's love test to some person or group who claims to be speaking for God. Does that person or group show active love for Christians?
   b. Apply the love test to yourself.

Optional Application: God's love for us cost Him His Son. Christ's love for us cost Him His life. What would it cost you to love someone you need to love?

4:10 _____

_____

4:14 _____

_____

2. What does this tell you about God's kind of love?

_____

_____

_____

_____

3. "No one has ever seen God" (1 John 4:12), for He is a holy and incomprehensible Spirit (Exodus 33:18-20, John 4:24). How, then, can people come to see what He is like (1 John 4:12)? (*Optional:* Compare John 13:35, 17:20-21.)

_____

_____

_____

_____

Made complete . . . perfect (1 John 4:12,17-18). Perfect or complete love in this mortal life is not flawless love, but rather love that "reaches its intended goal and is fully developed when it produces the fruit of loving action toward others."[1]

4. If God's love is made complete in us, what are some of the results?

4:17 _____

_____

4:18 _____

_____

5. Why does perfect or completed love drive out
our fears about Judgment Day and punishment
(4:17-18)?

_____

_____

_____

_____

_____

6. a. What are some of your fears about God, other
people, and circumstances? (See, for example,
Luke 12:1-12,22-34.)

_____

_____

_____

_____

_____

_____

b. How can 1 John 4:7-18 help you let go of
those fears? (How does perfect love drive
them out?) Pray about this. You might ask
others to pray, too.

_____

_____

_____

_____

_____

_____

For Thought and Discussion: a. Have you been in any way healed or strengthened because someone has chosen not to be offended by you or has made some sacrifice for you?

b. How has experiencing love affected your ability to love others?

For Thought and Discussion: Why does being like God in the world give us confidence regarding Judgment Day (4:17)?

For Thought and Discussion: In what ways does fear have to do with punishment?

Optional Application: How can you let God's love be made complete in you this week? Or, how can you let your fears be driven out as you love others this week?

For Thought and Discussion: Why isn't it easier to love God, who is perfect, than your brother, who is imperfect (4:20-21)?

c. How might your choices and actions be different if you weren't afraid?

_____

_____

_____

_____

Fear (4:18). This word has a wide range of meaning in Scripture. On the one hand, "The fear of the LORD is the beginning of wisdom" (Proverbs 9:10; compare Psalm 34:6-14 and 1 Peter 2:17). On the other hand, believers who are actively seeking to obey God and love people need not be terrified of God. For other good and bad fears, see Luke 12:1-12,22-34.

---

7. Why is it impossible to love God without loving other believers?

4:20 _____

_____

4:21 _____

_____

5:1 _____

_____

8. "We love because he first loved us" (4:19). Why does God loving us lead to our loving others?

_____

_____

_____

_____

_____

9. Looking back over 4:7-5:1, list John's reasons why Christians love other Christians.

_____

_____

_____

_____

_____

_____

10. Read the optional questions in this lesson. What truth in 4:7-5:1 seems most relevant to you?

_____

_____

_____

11. How has this truth already begun to affect your life?

_____

_____

_____

_____

12. How would you like to grow in this area?

_____

_____

_____

_____

_____

For Thought and Discussion: a. Why does knowing we are loved drive out our fear?

b. Why does letting God's love flow actively through us to others drive out our fear?

For Further Study: Add 4:1-6 (from lesson six) and 4:7-5:1 to your outline. Or, wait until you are done with 5:2-12, since 4:7-5:5 is a unified section.

99

13. What action can you take this week to put this truth into practice?

_____

_____

_____

_____

_____

14. List any questions you have about 4:7-5:1.

_____

_____

_____

_____

For the group

First John 4:7-5:5 is a unified passage, but in order to make lessons nine and ten of even length, we have ended lesson nine with 5:1. It is a somewhat arbitrary place to break, but you will go back and look at all of 4:7-5:5 in lesson ten.

Warm-up. Recall one recent time when someone put up with your faults or sacrificed his or her desires for your needs. How did the experience affect you?

Questions. The focus of this lesson is on why and how God's love for us moves us to love other believers. Are we motivated by gratitude, moral obligation, God's direct command. . . ? Does God love through us, do we imitate His love, or both? What is God's kind of love?

The phrase "perfect love drives out fear" (4:18) can be interpreted in many ways—some true, some not. (Is it our love, God's love for us, God loving through us? Is it our fear being driven out, or the loved person's fear, or both?) The teaching of the rest of Scripture should guide you in discerning true from false interpretations. If you are unsure about an interpretation, consult commentaries or a Christian who is well-versed in the Bible.

After sharing some of your fears, pray for each other to be free of them. Ask God to make His love complete in those of you with fear. Explore ways each of you can act out God's kind of love for one another and other believers.

Worship. Praise the God who is love. Thank Him for sending His Son to save the world, atone for our sins, and give us life. Thank Him for dwelling in you and making His love complete in you as you pour it out to others. Thank Him that perfect love drives out all your fears.

1. Burdick, page 333.

1 JOHN 5:1-12

Testimony

*"He who has the Son has life; he who does not
have the Son of God does not have life."*
                              1 John 5:12

First John 4:7-5:5 is really all one section in which
John interweaves his ethical and doctrinal tests—
obedience, love, and faith in Christ. Then, 5:6-12
deals more specifically with the doctrine of Christ.
As you read 5:1-12, look for the connections
between obedience, love, faith in Jesus Christ, and
being born of God (having eternal life).

Obedience, love, and faith (5:1-5)

Believes (5:1,5). As 2:23; 4:2-3,15; and 5:10 make
    clear, it is not enough just to give intellectual
    assent to the idea that Jesus is the Christ. Belief
    includes personal commitment, public acknowl-
    edgment despite opposition, and trust. We don't
    just believe facts *about* Jesus; we believe *in* Him
    as our personal Lord and Savior (5:10).[1]

1. Explain how at least three of the following pairs
   are related to each other:

   loving God and obeying God (2:15-17, 5:2-3)

_____

_____

_____

_____

loving God and loving other believers (4:20-5:2)

_____

_____

_____

_____

obeying God and loving other believers (3:23,
4:21)

_____

_____

_____

_____

believing in Jesus and loving other believers
(3:16; 4:9-11,15,19; 5;1)

_____

_____

_____

_____

believing in Jesus and loving/obeying God

_____

_____

_____

_____

_____

being born of God and righteousness/
obedience/love/belief (3:10,23-24; 5:1)

_____

_____

_____

_____

_____

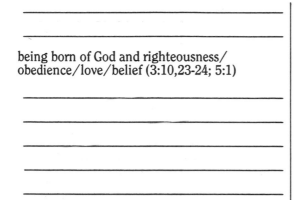

Study Skill—Diagrams
A picture sometimes helps to clarify connections between ideas. The diagram below is an
attempt to portray the relationships among
righteousness, obedience, love, belief, and
rebirth as John describes them. You might
find a better way to depict these connections.

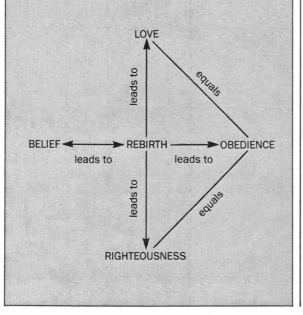

For Thought and Discussion: What does it mean to overcome the world (5:3-5)? See 2:16 and 3:7-10.

Optional Application: What evidence of love for God or overcoming the world does your life show?

For Thought and Discussion: How does our faith overcome the world?

2. Why are God's commands (including love) not burdensome for those who are born of Him (5:3-5)? Explain in your own words.

_____

_____

_____

_____

_____

3. What personal lessons can you draw from 5:1-5?

_____

_____

_____

_____

_____

_____

_____

Three witnesses (5:6-12)

Testifies, testimony (5:6-11). These words ("witness" in NASB) occur ten times in 5:6-11. Jewish law requires two or three witnesses to confirm the facts in a legal case (Deuteronomy 19:15). John says that there are ample witnesses testifying to the fact that Jesus is both God and man.

Water and blood (5:6). There are several interpretations of these, and some people think John has more than one meaning in mind.
    1. *Baptism and the Lord's Supper.*
    2. *The piercing of Jesus' side at the Crucifixion* (John 19:34).
    3. *Christ's baptism and death.* The Gnostic Cerinthus taught that the divine Christ entered the man Jesus at his baptism and left him just

before his death. John agrees that Jesus' baptism marked the beginning of His public ministry. But John insists that the Christ was still being manifested in the world in Jesus' death. The blood of crucifixion was the Christ's blood, just as the water of Jesus' baptism was His.[2]

The Spirit (5:6). (5:7 in NASB and RSV.) At Jesus' baptism, the Spirit descended on Him as a dove (Matthew 3:16), and John the Baptist later said that this proved Jesus was the Christ (John 1:31-34). The Spirit continues to witness to Jesus' identity through the Scriptures and inner conviction (John 15:26, 16:8-11).[3]

Water, blood, and the Holy Spirit all witness to the fact that Jesus is, and always has been, the divine Christ.

For Thought and Discussion: What is a person saying about God when he rejects the Bible's testimony about Jesus (5:10)? Why?

For Further Study: For more on the inner testimony (1 John 5:10), see Romans 8:16, 2 Corinthians 1:21-22, Galatians 4:6, Ephesians 1:13-14, 1 John 4:13.

4. We accept the testimony of three human witnesses in a trial. Why is God's testimony— through the Spirit, the water, and the blood— even more trustworthy (5:9)?

_____

_____

_____

_____

_____

5. What is God's testimony through the three witnesses (5:11-12)?

_____

_____

_____

_____

_____

6. God testified to Jesus during His lifetime and continues to testify to those historical facts through the Bible. What happens to God's tes-

Optional Application: a. What are the keys to overcoming the world's compulsion to fear, lust, pride, hatred, depression, etc.? (See 2:14-17, 5:4-5.)
b. How can you apply these insights so as to overcome the world?

timony when a person puts his faith in Jesus (5:10)?

_____

_____

_____

_____

7. What convinced (and convinces) you that Jesus is God's Son and the source of eternal life?

_____

_____

_____

_____

_____

_____

8. How are water, blood, and the Spirit related to your reasons for faith?

_____

_____

_____

_____

_____

_____

9. What insight from 5:1-12 seems most important to you currently?

_____

_____

_____

_____

_____

10. How is it relevant to you, or how do you want it to affect your life?

_____

_____

_____

_____

_____

_____

11. What action can you take to make this truth part of your life this week?

_____

_____

_____

_____

_____

_____

12. List any questions you have about 5:1-12.

_____

_____

_____

_____

_____

For Thought and Discussion: Is the inner witness of God in the heart as reliable as the objective witness of the water and the blood? Why or why not? How does each witness support and balance the other?

For Further Study: Complete your outline up through 5:1-12.

For the group

Warm-up. Ask each person to share one experience, statement, story in the Bible, or other reason that convinced him or her to believe in Jesus.

Obedience, love, and faith. It may be tedious to plow through all the pairs in question 1. You can cover just a few of them. Or, discuss what the diagram on page 105 portrays. Then discuss what personal lessons you each drew from these connections and how you might apply them.

Three witnesses. Make sure that everyone understands what the witnesses of the water, the blood, and the Spirit may be. Ask group members to explain the testimony of 5:11-12 in their own words. Then relate your own reasons for belief to the reasons John gives. How are they similar and different?

Worship. Thank God for giving His testimony through historical events, the Scripture, and the inner witness in each of you. Thank Him for giving you eternal life in His Son. Ask Him to convince you all fully of the truths about Jesus and eternal life. Meditate together on these truths and their implications—loving God's other children, obeying Him, and overcoming the world by faith in God's Son.

1. Burdick, pages 295, 342, 374-375.
2. Burdick, pages 365-368; Stott, pages 177-179.
3. Burdick, page 368.

1 JOHN 5:13-21

Assurance

"I write these things to you who believe in the name of the Son of God so that you may know that you have eternal life."
            1 John 5:13

Throughout his letter, John has unfolded tests by which we may recognize who is and isn't a Christian. He has done this partly in order to refute some false teachers trying to mislead his flock. But as 5:13-21 makes clear, the tests were also meant to reassure true believers. Two Greek words for "know" occur seven times in these verses. As you read the conclusion to John's letter, observe what John wants us to know with certainty.

1. Write down at least six things that John wants us to know or be assured of in 5:13-21. Then tell why each one is especially important for you to be certain of.

   a. _____

   _____

   _____

   _____

   _____

   _____

   _____

For Thought and Discussion: How can we come to know God's will and so have our prayers answered (5:14-15)? See, for example, John 15:7.

For Thought and Discussion: What kinds of things tempt you to doubt that you have eternal life, that God hears and answers your prayers, that Jesus keeps you from sin, etc.?

b. _____

_____

_____

_____

_____

_____

c. _____

_____

_____

_____

_____

_____

d. _____

_____

_____

_____

_____

_____

e. _____

_____

_____

_____

_____

_____

f. _____

_____

_____

_____

_____

_____

_____

Brother commit a sin (5:16). In 3:9 and 5:18 John
says that no one born of God sins (present
tense). Now John says we might well see a
brother committing a sin (present tense again).
Since "brother" has meant a believer everywhere else in this letter (2:9-11, 3:14-15, and
the emphasis on family relationship in 5:1), it
seems that John is talking about a genuine
Christian practicing some sin. Is this a
contradiction?

No. A child of God may commit individual
acts of sin (2:1). He may even have a habit of
committing some particular kind of sin over and
over—one that "does not lead to death" (5:16).
But he cannot have a lifestyle characterized by
habitual sin (3:9, 5:18).[1]

Give him life (5:16). If by "brother" John means a
believer, then he already has eternal life. In this
case, God will restore to him abundant life, the
experience of living intimately with God here
and now.[2]

If "brother" does not mean a real believer,
then this passage promises that God will give an
unbeliever eternal life in response to the Christian's prayer, provided that the unbeliever has
not committed the ***sin that leads to death.***[3]

Leads to death (5:16). The word translated "leads
to" means "moving in the direction of"—a tendency, not a definitely determined outcome.[4]
This sin has been interpreted as:

1. *One that leads to physical death.* First
Corinthians 11:30 says that God sometimes

For Thought and Discussion: In 5:16, does John mean that we shouldn't pray for those who commit sins leading to death? Or does he mean that we may, but a positive result isn't guaranteed?

For Thought and Discussion: Compare 3:9 to 5:18. Why doesn't the child of God practice sin?

gives a sinning Christian sickness or death as punishment, but there is not necessarily a loss of eternal life.

2. *One that leads a Christian to spiritual death.* This verse is cited by those who believe that a person can lose his salvation through serious sin.

3. *One that leads an unbeliever to irrevocable death.* The unbeliever is already spiritually dead (Ephesians 2:1); this sin makes that death permanent. Notice that John says a brother may commit a sin that does not lead to death, but he doesn't say whether or not a brother (a real believer) may commit a sin leading to death.[5]

Matthew 12:22-32 tells us the one unforgivable sin that certainly leads to spiritual death. It is blasphemy against the Holy Spirit: beholding God at work, knowing it is God at work, and rejecting Him by calling His work the work of Satan. The person who does this turns good and evil upside-down and refuses repentance and forgiveness.

---

2. In 5:16-17 John gives an example of 5:14-15—a prayer that is in accord with God's will. Explain in your own words what this prayer is that we can pray with assurance.

_____

_____

_____

_____

_____

_____

3. Do you know any brother indulging in a sin that does not lead to death? If so, pray for him or her.

The one who was born of God (5:18). Jesus, the unique Son of God.

Understanding (5:20). This Greek word means the capacity to understand spiritual things and know God personally.[6]

Him who is true (5:20). John contrasts the God Who is True with the dozens of *idols* (5:21) in cities throughout the Roman world. Ephesus housed literally hundreds of idols in temples large and small. The temple of Ephesian Artemis was one of the Seven Wonders of the World and drew tourists from all over the Empire. Idolatry was woven into daily life: meat came from temple butchers, dinner parties were often held in temples, civil servants had religious duties, and public festivals were all organized around cults. Avoiding idolatry was as difficult in John's day as avoiding the lure of money, sex, and power in the modern world. In addition, there was the danger of the Gnostics' false portrait of God, which was as bad as an idol.

Optional Application: How can you overcome the temptations of the idols you listed in question 4? What practical steps can you take this week?

For Further Study: Finish your outline of 1 John by adding 5:13-21.

4. What are some of the "idols" that tempt you to live apart from the true God?

_____

_____

_____

_____

_____

_____

5. Is there any truth in 5:13-21 that you especially want to meditate on, take to heart, and apply? If so, what is it and what do you want to do about it?

_____

_____

_____

_____

_____

_____

_____

_____

_____

6. Write down any questions you have about
   5:13-21.

_____

_____

_____

_____

For the group

Warm-up. Ask everyone to think of one prayer he or
she very much wants God to answer.

Questions. There are few questions in this lesson
because question 1 is so long. Spend a good portion
of your time really getting a grip on these assurances that John thinks are so important. Dig for
reasons why these are significant for each of you
personally.

Come to your own conclusions about the
meaning of 5:16. Then, if you can do it without
naming names, share the concerns you prayed about
in question 3. Try to find a way of praying together
about these concerns without betraying anyone's
privacy. Also, share your personal temptations
toward idolatry and plan to pray about these at the
end of your meeting. Finally, discuss any other
plans you each have for applying 5:13-21.

Worship. Praise the God Who is True. Thank Him
for each of the assurances John names. Ask Jesus to
keep you from sin, especially the specific idolatries
that tempt you. Pray for any brothers in danger of
committing sins.

1. Burdick, pages 389-390, 401-402. Stott thinks that "brother" in 5:16 means any nonbeliever, especially someone who belongs to the church but by his sinful habit reveals that he is not a child of God. See Stott, page 190.
2. Burdick, page 404; Marshall, pages 249-250, note 27.
3. Stott, page 190.
4. Burdick, page 390.
5. Burdick, pages 402-404.
6. J. Behm, *"dianoia"* in Gerhard Kittel and Gerhard Friedrich, *Theological Dictionary of the New Testament*, volume 4, translated by Geoffrey W. Bromiley (Grand Rapids, Michigan: William B. Eerdmans Publishing Company, 1968), page 967; Burdick, page 394.

REVIEW OF 1 JOHN

After studying 1 John in detail, do you have a grasp
of the book as a whole? If your head is full of a jum-
ble of details and individual verses, a review can
help you sort out what you've learned.

1. First, reread all of 1 John. It should be familiar
   by now, so you should be able to read quickly to
   observe themes that run through the letter.
   Pray for a fresh perspective on what God is saying. (A different translation than the one you've
   been using might be illuminating.)

2. What is the letter about? What were John's
   goals in writing it?

   _____

   _____

   _____

   _____

   _____

   _____

   _____

3. If you haven't already made an outline, you can
   use the blank pages at the end of this study
   guide to make one now. Use the outline on
   pages 16-17 as a framework, or devise your own.

For Further Study:
Compare John's
explanations of love
to Paul's in 1 Corin-
thians 13.

**For Thought and
Discussion:** Why
don't Christians prac-
tice habitual sin?

4. What are John's tests by which we may discern
   who is and isn't a child of God?

   _____

   _____

   _____

   _____

   _____

5. What is Christian love, according to John
   (2:7-11, 3:11-24, 4:7-21)? What does he want us
   to know about it?

   _____

   _____

   _____

   _____

   _____

   _____

6. What does it mean to "acknowledge that Jesus
   Christ has come in the flesh" (4:2) and to
   "believe in the Son of God" (5:10)?

   _____

   _____

   _____

   _____

   _____

   _____

7. Review the questions you listed at the ends of
   lessons one through eleven. Do any of them
   remain unanswered? If so, some of the sources
   on pages 143-147 may help you. You might plan
   to study some particular passage further with
   cross-references on your own.

120

8. Have you noticed any areas (thoughts, attitudes, behavior) in which you have changed as a result of studying 1 John? If so, how have you changed?

_____

_____

_____

_____

_____

_____

For Thought and Discussion: a. What have you learned from John's letter about answers to prayer (3:21-23, 5:13-17)?

b. What have you learned about overcoming sin?

9. Look back over the study at questions in which you expressed a desire to make some specific application. Are you satisfied with your follow-through and the results of your efforts? Pray about any areas that you think you should continue to pursue.

What topic (or topics) continue to challenge you personally, and what do you plan to do about it?

_____

_____

_____

_____

_____

_____

_____

_____

For the group

Read aloud. If you feel that it would take too long to read all of 1 John, have someone read just 1:1-2:28. This is the section you studied longest ago, and it should be enough to refresh everyone's memories.

Questions. Discuss questions 2, 4, 5, and 6 along with any of the optional questions that cover themes you think are particularly important. Review what John says about each topic and also how it is relevant to your lives.

Let group members ask any questions they still have about the book. Try to have other group members give answers, or suggest sources of answers to complicated questions. Often, if a leader gives answers himself or herself, then the group never outgrows dependence on the leader.

Review your progress in applying John's words. How have you grown? How could you have done better? Let members tell what growth they see in each other. You might plan some further applications as a group. Let your goal here be to encourage group members to improve in application by relying on God's strength, priorities, and timing. Competition, despair, and indifference should be dealt with if observed.

Worship. Thank God for the specific things He has taught you and the specific ways He has changed you through your study of 1 John. Thank Him also for the opportunity to study the Bible together.

2 JOHN 1-13

Love and Truth

Hospitality

The Romans knew that a prosperous, united empire needed a way for people to travel safely. So, they invested a lot of money and effort in building roads and guarding them from bandits. The stone high-ways were smooth and wide enough for soldiers to get to trouble spots quickly. And while robbers and wild animals were not eliminated in lonely areas, they were curbed enough to let civilians travel with some security.

And civilians did travel. Not only merchants and government officials, but tourists, pilgrims, magicians, priests of every cult, and teachers of every imaginable doctrine walked or rode from Syria to Spain and back again. A teacher of grammar, rhetoric, or philosophy would arrive in a town and try to attract paying students among the sons of local men. Religious missionaries sought adoration (and money) for their deities and doctrines. Among all these the evangelists of Jesus Christ traveled, doing their best to stand out from the competition as the messengers of truth.

There were inns every twenty-two miles or so along the Roman roads, but they were no place for respectable people. "The average inn was no more than a courtyard surrounded by rooms. Baggage was piled in the open space, where animals were also tethered for the night. . . . [In a room the] snorting and stamping of the animals outside was sometimes drowned out by the snores of others who shared the room, any one of whom might be a thief."[1] If one's bedmate was not a robber, the innkeeper certainly was, and if some men could sleep without fear of theft, few could endure the plague of fleas.

Therefore, people tried to stay with friends of friends when they traveled. And because the spread of the gospel depended on missionaries, hospitality was considered one of the chief expressions of Christian love (Romans 12:13, Hebrews 13:2). Paul often stayed with converts while he was in a town (Acts 13-21). Likewise, he asked believers to house messengers and teachers, and to help them with provisions for the next leg of their journeys when they left (Romans 15:23-24, 16:1-2; Titus 3:12-13).

But when it became known that Christians would feed and house anyone who claimed to be a teacher of the gospel, unscrupulous people began to take advantage. *The Didache*, a manual for Syrian churches, written about the same time as 2 and 3 John, gave guidelines for Christian hospitality (see pages 131-133). The churches John was overseeing in Asia Minor were running into similar problems, and the apostle wrote 2 and 3 John to address them.

Advice for the lady

Study Skill—An Epistle's Purpose
An epistle is a letter. People usually write letters in response to a particular situation in their own and their readers' lives. This is less obvious in longer biblical epistles, but it is easy to see in 2 and 3 John. Although they are inspired Scripture for all time, they are also ordinary letters. Even though we can't reconstruct the exact circumstances John was writing about, we will understand his (and the Holy Spirit's) message better if we can discern something about those circumstances.

Before studying any epistle, it is a good idea to read it once, asking yourself, "What is this letter about? What situation seems to have prompted the writer to send it in the first place?" Later, when you seek to apply
(continued on page 125)

(continued from page 124)
the epistle's teaching to yourself, you will ask, "How is my situation like and unlike the one this letter's first readers were in? How do the letter's words to them apply to me in my circumstances?"

Historical background like that given above is invaluable in reconstructing the original situation. Still, your main clues will be found by reading and re-reading the letter itself.

1. Read 2 John. What is the letter about? What situation does John seem to be addressing?

_____

_____

_____

_____

_____

_____

The elder (verse 1). Tradition records that John spent his later years in Ephesus. At more than eighty years of age, he was probably the oldest and most respected Christian leader in the province. He may also have served as an official elder of the Ephesian church. "The elder" was apparently a title of loving respect by which the churches of Asia knew John.[2]

The chosen lady (verse 1). She may have been a well-to-do woman in one of the churches of Asia. Or, this phrase may be a way of describing a church. Israel in the Old Testament and the Church in the New Testament are often portrayed as women (Isaiah 52:2, 54:1-4, 62:4-5; Ephesians 5:22-33; Revelation 21:9). Some people feel that the language of this letter applies better to a church than to a family, but in fact it applies to both equally well. The lady **and**

125

her children may be a family offering their house to missionaries as Lydia did (Acts 16:14-15). Or, they may be a church and its members offering hospitality and an official welcome to teach.[3]

Truth (verses 1-4). "The truth embodied in the gospel."[4]

Grace, mercy and peace (verse 3). Unlike 1 John, 2 John begins more like a typical Greek letter: The elder to the lady, greetings (compare Acts 15:23, James 1:1). A Greek would write "greetings" (*chairein*), while a Jew would write "peace." Paul passed to the rest of the Church the habit of saying "grace" (*charis*) and "peace" (1 Corinthians 1:3). To Timothy, Paul wrote "grace, mercy and peace" (1 Timothy 1:2, 2 Timothy 1:2). But while Paul's greeting was a prayer for his readers, John says that grace, mercy, and peace *will be with us*.

Grace is "the unmerited favor of God to sinful man."[5] Mercy is "compassionate treatment of an offender, enemy, etc."[6] Peace is well-being in all areas of life because of God's presence.[7]

---

2. John repeats "truth" five times in verses 1-4. What does he say about the truth?

verse 1 _____

_____

verse 1 _____

_____

verse 2 _____

_____

verse 3 _____

_____

verse 4 _____

_____

3. John also has a lot to say about love in verses 1-6. What does he say about love?

verse 1 _____

_____

verse 3 _____

_____

verse 5 _____

_____

verse 6 _____

_____

Optional Application: Are you walking in truth, obedience, and love? How does your life reflect this? How can you improve in this area?

4. What does it mean to *walk* in the truth (as opposed to believing it intellectually)?

_____

_____

_____

_____

5. Why do you think John so emphasizes *walking* in truth, obedience, and love?

_____

_____

_____

_____

_____

Jesus Christ as coming in the flesh (verse 7). Compare 1 John 4:2-3. This is John's doctrinal test. The present tense "coming" implies that the human and divine natures were united in Jesus at His conception and have never ceased to be united.[8]

127

Rewarded fully (verse 8). "The thought is not of their winning or losing their salvation (which is a free gift), but their reward for faithful service."[9] (Compare Mark 9:41, 10:29-30; Luke 19:11-19; Hebrews 11:26.)

Runs ahead (verse 9). The deceivers thought they were being progressive and sophisticated in adjusting the doctrine of Christ, in disposing of the distasteful idea that divine spirit could unite with corrupt matter. However, this kind of "progress" is not toward, but away from, truth. To *continue* in truth is not sterile conservatism, but sanity.

Take him into your house or welcome him (verse 10). These Greek idioms refer to housing someone, providing a base for him, and giving your blessing when he leaves.[10]

If "the chosen lady" is a church, then "your house" is the home or building where the church meets. In that case, John is also warning against giving an official welcome and a platform for teaching.[11]

The children of your chosen sister (verse 13). Either the children of the lady's biological sister or the members of the sister church from which John was writing.

6. In contrast to those who are walking in the truth, some people are walking in error. Describe their error in your own words (verses 7,9).

_____

_____

_____

_____

_____

_____

_____

7. Why is this error so abhorrent to John?

_____

_____

_____

_____

Optional Application: How are you walking in love toward Christian teachers who visit your church or area? How can you do more of this?

8. One expression of love that was expected of Christians was hospitality. Would it be consist ent with Christian love and truth to give hospi- tality to teachers of the falsehood you just de- scribed? Why or why not (verses 10-11)?

_____

_____

_____

_____

_____

9. What happens when we try to walk in love without truth (verses 8,11)?

_____

_____

_____

_____

10. What happens when we try to walk in truth without love?

_____

_____

_____

_____

Optional Application: Are there any teachers in your area benefiting from Christian support but subtly undermining Christian truth? If so, how can you see that you and others are not deceived into helping them?

11. Do verses 10-11 mean that Christians should neither speak to nor have in their homes anyone whose beliefs are not perfectly Christian? Why or why not?

_____

_____

_____

_____

_____

_____

_____

12. Do verses 10-11 mean that Christians should stop feeding, housing, and giving official church welcomes to all traveling teachers, for fear they might accidentally aid false ones? Why or why not (verse 6)?

_____

_____

_____

_____

_____

13. You've looked at 2 John in its original situation, and you've drawn from it some abiding principles for Christian practice. Now, how is this letter personally relevant to you?

_____

_____

_____

_____

_____

_____

14. What steps can you take to put this teaching into practice?

_____

_____

_____

_____

_____

15. List any questions you have about 2 John.

_____

_____

_____

_____

Optional Application: a. How are you showing love toward other members of your fellowship, church, or small group? How can you do this in new ways?

b. Are there any threats to unity, love, and truth in your group? If so, what can you do about them?

For the group

Warm-up. Ask everyone to think of one opportunity he or she has had in the past week to act with love toward another Christian.

Worship. Thank God for the true missionaries of the gospel, for the ability to discern true teachers from false ones, for ways those around you are treating you with love, and for their example of walking in the truth.

The Didache

Around the time John was writing letters to churches in Asia, the churches in Syria were formulating a manual of guidelines for such matters as baptism, fasting, the Lord's Supper, traveling missionaries, local ministers, and so on. It was called *The Lord's Teaching to the Heathen by the Twelve Apostles,* and modern scholars call it *The Didache* (Greek for "The Teaching") for short. *The Didache* (pronounced *did-a-kay*) is not inspired Scripture, but it does show us how one group of churches was handling the same
(continued on page 132)

(continued from page 131)

kinds of situations that John's churches were facing. Here are some excerpts:[12]

"Now about the apostles and prophets: Act in line with the gospel precept [Matthew 10:40-41]. Welcome every apostle on arriving, as if he were the Lord. But he must not stay beyond one day. In case of necessity, however, the next day too. If he stays three days, he is a false prophet. On departing, an apostle must not accept anything save sufficient food to carry him till his next lodging. If he asks for money, he is a false prophet.

"While a prophet is making ecstatic utterances [literally, 'speaking in a spirit'], you must not test or examine him. For 'every sin will be forgiven,' but this sin 'will not be forgiven' [Matthew 12:31]. However, not everybody making ecstatic utterances is a prophet, but only if he behaves like the Lord. It is by their conduct that the false prophet and the [true] prophet can be distinguished. For instance, if a prophet marks out a table in the Spirit, he must not eat from it. If he does, he is a false prophet. Again, every prophet who teaches the truth but fails to practice what he preaches is a false prophet. But every attested and genuine prophet who acts with a view to symbolizing the mystery of the Church, and does not teach you to do all he does, must not be judged by you. His judgment rests with God. For the ancient prophets too acted in this way. But if someone says in the Spirit, 'Give me money, or something else,' you must not heed him. However, if he tells you to give for others in need, no one must condemn him.

"Everyone 'who comes' to you 'in the name of the Lord' must be welcomed. Afterward, when you have tested him, you will find out about him, for you have insight into right and wrong. If it is a traveler who arrives, help him all you can. But he must not stay with you more than two days, or, if necessary, three. If he wants to settle with you and is an artisan, he must work for his living. If, however, he has no trade, use your

(continued on page 133)

(continued from page 132)
judgment in taking steps for him to live with you as a Christian without being idle. If he refuses to do this, he is trading on Christ. You must be on your guard against such people.

"Every genuine prophet who wants to settle with you 'has a right to his support.' Similarly, a genuine teacher himself, just like a 'workman, has a right to his support' [Matthew 10:10]. Hence take all the first fruits of vintage and harvest, and of cattle and sheep, and give these first fruits to the prophets. For they are your high priests. If, however, you have no prophet, give them to the poor. . . ."

1. Jerome Murphy-O'Connor, "On the Road and on the Sea with St. Paul," *Bible Review* (Washington, D. C.: Biblical Archaeology Society, Summer 1985), page 42.
2. Burdick, pages 13-16.
3. Burdick, pages 415-417; Stott, pages 200-202.
4. Burdick, page 420.
5. Burdick, page 421.
6. *The American Heritage Dictionary of the English Language* (New York: Dell Publishing Company, 1969), page 443.
7. Hartmut Beck and Colin Brown, "Peace," *The New International Dictionary of New Testament Theology*, volume 2, pages 776-783.
8. Stott, pages 209-210.
9. Stott, page 210.
10. Burdick, pages 428-429.
11. Stott, pages 212-214.
12. *The Didache*, in *Early Christian Fathers*, translated by Cyril C. Richardson (New York: Macmillan Publishing Company, 1970), pages 161-179. The excerpts are from sections 11-13, pages 176-178.

3 JOHN 1-14

Love and Rebellion

In your zeal to show love to traveling Christians, John wrote to the lady, don't compromise truth by aiding teachers of falsehood. Your love is commendable, but it must be wedded to truth. The situation in Gaius' church is different. So, although the issue is still hospitality, John's praise and warning in 3 John reflect another facet of this act of love.

1. Read 3 John. What is it about? Describe the situation John seems to be addressing.

_____

_____

_____

_____

_____

_____

Gaius (verse 1). A common name at that time. Three other men are named Gaius in the New Testament, but this man seems to be none of them.[1]

I pray that (verse 2). It was customary to follow a greeting with a prayer for the reader's welfare. John's prayer has an explicitly Christian focus.

**For Thought and
Discussion:** a. How
is 3 John like and
unlike 2 John?
(Observe the repeti-
tion and change of
various phrases and
topics.)
b. What themes
does each letter have
in common with
1 John? What does
this tell you about
John's priorities?

**For Thought and
Discussion:** a. Which
of the three possible
meanings of "in a
manner worthy of
God" do you think
John had in mind?
b. What do you
think "for the sake of
the Name" means
(verse 7)? See Philip-
pians 2:9-11.

Some brothers (verse 3). Probably Christian
teachers traveling through Asia. The Greek verb
tenses of *come* and *tell* imply that travelers were
coming to Ephesus repeatedly and telling John
about the welcome Gaius had given them.[2]

2. What does John pray for Gaius (verse 2)?

_____

_____

_____

_____

_____

3. What good things has John heard about Gaius?

verse 2 _____

_____

_____

verse 3 _____

_____

_____

_____

Faithful (verse 5). "Trustworthy, dependable,
loyal."[3]

Send them on their way (verse 6). "Something of a
technical term among early Christians for the
act of providing the traveller with goods for his
journey."[4] There were no restaurants or stores
along the road, so a person had to carry his food
(and often his drink) with him.

A manner worthy of God (verse 6). This could mean
a) God's messengers should be treated the way
God should be treated (Matthew 10:40); b) we
should treat others the way God has treated us;

136

or c) as God's representatives, we should treat others in the way that will bring praise to God (Colossians 1:10, 1 Thessalonians 2:12).[5]

4. How has Gaius been showing faithfulness, and how should he continue to do so (verses 5-8)? Explain in your own words.

_____

_____

_____

_____

_____

_____

Optional Application: How are you showing faithfulness to the truth in what you are doing for other Christians? How can you do this in new ways? What opportunities do your circumstances offer?

Optional Application: How can you "work together for the truth" with missionaries and teachers? Is hospitality an option? What other ways of providing support could you practice?

5. Why is this such an important ministry (verse 8)?

_____

_____

_____

_____

_____

Diotrephes (verse 9). We don't know if he was an official elder of the church or just a member usurping power. In either case, he was misusing his influence in order to grasp dictatorial power for himself.

6. How is Diotrephes doing exactly the opposite of what John commends Gaius for doing (verses 9-10)?

_____

_____

137

For Thought and Discussion: Why would a person like Diotrephes object to visiting teachers, John's authority, and Gaius' refusal to bow to his will?

Optional Application: Do you show any signs of loving to be first? Pray about this, and confess if necessary. How can you let God uproot and guard against this fault?

_____
_____
_____
_____

7. What do you think it means to love to be first (verse 9)?

_____
_____
_____
_____
_____

Does what is good (verse 11). The Greek tense implies a continual practice, not occasional good deeds.

8. How is the general exhortation in verse 11 relevant to the situation Gaius faces in his church?

_____
_____
_____
_____
_____

Demetrius (verse 12). Probably the man who carried this letter from John to Gaius. (There was no civilian postal system, so letters were always carried by messengers.) One of John's reasons for writing this letter may have been to see that Gaius welcomed Demetrius despite Diotrephes' opposition.[6]

9. How can "the truth" (verse 12) speak well of someone?

_____

_____

_____

_____

_____

10. How are John's attitudes in 3 John examples for every pastor?

_____

_____

_____

_____

_____

11. Now that you've looked at this letter in detail, summarize again what it is about. What main lessons or principles does it convey?

_____

_____

_____

_____

_____

_____

_____

12. What one truth in this letter seems most personally relevant to you?

_____

_____

_____

For Thought and Discussion: What do you learn about the scope of John's apostolic ministry from 2 and 3 John? Over whom did he have authority? How did he exercize his authority? How was his approach different from Diotrephes'?

Optional Application: Does your church or fellowship reflect any disunity like Gaius' church shows? What draws you together, and what is driving, or could drive, you apart? What can you do to heal those wounds?

_____

_____

13. How do you already see this truth active in your
    life?

    _____

    _____

    _____

    _____

    _____

14. How would you like your life to reflect this
    truth more than it already is?

    _____

    _____

    _____

    _____

    _____

15. What steps can you take to cooperate with God
    in achieving this? How can you put this truth
    more into practice this week?

    _____

    _____

    _____

    _____

    _____

16. List any questions you have about 3 John.

    _____

    _____

    _____

    _____

For the group

Warm-up. Ask everyone to think of one thing he or she is doing to work with other Christians for the truth of the gospel. If some group members can't think of anything, don't condemn them. By the end of this lesson, try to see that each person has come up with one concrete way of working for the truth.

Questions. Your discussion goals should be:
1. What is this letter about? (What was the original situation?)
2. What abiding lessons or principles does it teach you?
3. How are these lessons personally relevant to you, and how can you apply them?

Worship. Thank God for the positive example of Gaius and the negative example of Diotrephes. Thank Him for all the Christians who are working together for the truth. Ask Him to involve you more as one of them.

Evaluation. Take a few minutes or a whole meeting to evaluate how your group functioned during your study of 1, 2, and 3 John. Here are some questions you might consider:

> How well did the study help you grasp 1, 2, and 3 John? Why?
> What were the most important truths you discovered together about the Lord?
> What did you like best about your meetings?
> What did you like least? What would you change?
> How well did you meet the goals you set at your first meeting?
> What did you learn about small group study?
> What are members' current needs and interests?
> What will you do next?

1. Burdick, page 443.
2. Burdick, page 448.
3. Burdick, page 450.
4. Burdick, page 451.
5. Burdick, page 451.
6. Burdick, page 458.

STUDY AIDS

For further information on the material covered in this study, consider the following sources. If your local bookstore does not have them, ask the bookstore to order them from the publisher, or find them in a seminary library. Many university and public libraries will also carry these books.

Commentaries on 1, 2, and 3 John

Boice, James Montgomery. *The Epistles of John: An Expositional Commentary* (Zondervan, 1979).
> This is a collection of Boice's sermons on John's letters. Along with some discussion of Greek word meanings and the cultural context, Boice deals mainly with what he thinks the text means and how it applies to modern people. Boice writes for the ordinary person with an eye to personal growth.

Burdick, Donald W. *The Letters of John the Apostle* (Moody Press, 1985).
> A thorough exegetical commentary for serious students. Burdick writes in clear English for the layperson or scholar, but he is dealing with the Greek text. Readers with no knowledge of Greek might get bogged down in the exegetical sections. However, Burdick's theological commentaries, modern applications, paraphrases, and outlines for each passage are kept separate from the Greek exegesis, so the non-Greek reader can still get a lot out of the book. Burdick examines most of the various interpretations of each passage and gives his own conclusions, so this one commentary is an in-depth introduction to the current scholarship on John's letters.

Stott, John R. W. *The Epistles of John* (Tyndale Series, Eerdmans, 1960).
> An older and somewhat less thorough commentary than Burdick's, but it deals with the English text for non-Greek readers. Stott's reflec-

tions remain stimulating and sound. Boice, Burdick, and Stott all capture John's pastoral feeling for his flock—their various backgrounds offer a well-rounded view.

Historical Sources

Bruce, F. F. *New Testament History* (Doubleday, 1979).
   A history of Herodian kings, Roman governors, philosophical schools, Jewish sects, Jesus, the early Jerusalem church, Paul, and early gentile Christianity.

Harrison, E. F. *Introduction to the New Testament* (Eerdmans, 1971).
   History from Alexander the Great—who made Greek culture dominant in the biblical world—through philosophies, pagan and Jewish religion, Jesus' ministry and teaching (the weakest section), and the spread of Christianity. Very good maps and photographs of the land, art, and architecture of New Testament times.

Concordances, Dictionaries, and Handbooks

A *concordance* lists words of the Bible alphabetically along with each verse in which the word appears. It lets you do your own word studies. An *exhaustive* concordance lists every word used in a given translation, while an *abridged* or *complete* concordance omits either some words, some occurrences of the word, or both.
   The two best exhaustive concordances are *Strong's Exhaustive Concordance* and *Young's Analytical Concordance to the Bible*. Both are available based on the King James Version of the Bible and the New American Standard Bible. *Strong's* has an index by which you can find out which Greek or Hebrew word is used in a given English verse. *Young's* breaks up each English word it translates. However, neither concordance requires knowledge of the original language.
   Among other good, less expensive concordances, *Cruden's Complete Concordance* is keyed to the King James and Revised Versions, and *The NIV Complete Concordance* is keyed to the New International Version. These include all references to every word included, but they omit "minor" words. They also lack indexes to the original languages.

A *Bible dictionary* or *Bible encyclopedia* alphabetically lists articles about people, places, doctrines, important words, customs, and geography of the Bible.
   The New Bible Dictionary, edited by J. D. Douglas, F. F. Bruce, J. I. Packer, N. Hillyer, D. Guthrie, A. R. Millard, and D. J. Wiseman (Tyndale, 1982) is more comprehensive than most dictionaries. Its 1300 pages include quantities of information along with excellent maps, charts, diagrams, and an index for cross-referencing.

Unger's Bible Dictionary by Merrill F. Unger (Moody, 1979) is equally good and is available in an inexpensive paperback edition.

The Zondervan Pictorial Encyclopedia edited by Merrill C. Tenney (Zondervan, 1975, 1976) is excellent and exhaustive, and is being revised and updated in the 1980s. However, its five 1000-page volumes are a financial investment, so all but very serious students may prefer to use it at a church, public, college, or seminary library.

Unlike a Bible dictionary in the above sense, *Vine's Expository Dictionary of New Testament Words* by W. E. Vine (various publishers) alphabetically lists major words used in the King James Version and defines each New Testament Greek word that KJV translates with that English word. *Vine's* lists verse references where that Greek word appears, so that you can do your own cross-references and word studies without knowing any Greek.

Vine's is a good basic book for beginners, but it is much less complete than other Greek helps for English speakers. More serious students might prefer *The New International Dictionary of New Testament Theology*, edited by Colin Brown (Zondervan) or *The Theological Dictionary of the New Testament* by Gerhard Kittel and Gerhard Friedrich, abridged in one volume by Geoffrey W. Bromiley (Eerdmans).

A *Bible atlas* can be a great aid to understanding what is going on in a book of the Bible and how geography affected events. Here are a few good choices:

The Macmillan Atlas by Yohanan Aharoni and Michael Avi-Yonah (Macmillan, 1968, 1977) contains 264 maps, 89 photos, and 12 graphics. The many maps of individual events portray battles, movements of people, and changing boundaries in detail.

The New Bible Atlas by J. J. Bimson and J. P. Kane (Tyndale, 1985) has 73 maps, 34 photos, and 34 graphics. Its evangelical perspective, concise and helpful text, and excellent research make it a very good choice, but its greatest strength is its outstanding graphics, such as cross-sections of the Dead Sea.

The Moody Atlas of Bible Lands by Barry J. Beitzel (Moody, 1984) is scholarly, very evangelical, and full of theological text, indexes, and references. This admirable reference work will be too deep and costly for some, but Beitzel shows vividly how God prepared the land of Israel perfectly for the acts of salvation He was going to accomplish in it.

A *handbook* of biblical customs can also be useful. Some good ones are *Today's Handbook of Bible Times and Customs* by William L. Coleman (Bethany, 1984), the less detailed *Daily Life in Bible Times* (Nelson, 1982), and *The New Manners and Customs of Bible Times* by Ralph Gower (Moody, 1987).

For Small Group Leaders

The Small Group Leader's Handbook by Steve Barker et al. (InterVarsity, 1982).

Written by an InterVarsity small group with college students primarily in mind. It includes more than the above book on small group dynamics and how to lead in light of them, and many ideas for worship, building community, and outreach. It has a good chapter on doing inductive Bible study.

Getting Together: A Guide for Good Groups by Em Griffin (InterVarsity, 1982).
Applies to all kinds of groups, not just Bible studies. From his own experience, Griffin draws deep insights into why people join groups; how people relate to each other; and principles of leadership, decision making, and discussions. It is fun to read, but its 229 pages will take more time than the above books.

You Can Start a Bible Study Group by Gladys Hunt (Harold Shaw, 1984).
Builds on Hunt's thirty years of experience leading groups. This book is wonderfully focused on God's enabling. It is both clear and applicable for Bible study groups of all kinds.

How to Lead Small Groups by Neal F. McBride (NavPress, 1990).
Covers leadership skills for all kinds of small groups—Bible study, fellowship, task, and support groups. Filled with step-by-step guidance and practical exercises to help you grasp the critical aspects of small group leadership and dynamics.

The Small Group Letter, a special section in *Discipleship Journal* (NavPress).
Unique. Its four pages per issue, six issues per year are packed with practical ideas for small groups. It stays up to date because writers discuss what they are currently doing as small group members and leaders. To subscribe, write to Subscription Services, Post Office Box 54470, Boulder, Colorado 80323-4470.

Bible Study Methods

Braga, James. *How to Study the Bible* (Multnomah, 1982).
Clear chapters on a variety of approaches to Bible study: synthetic, geographical, cultural, historical, doctrinal, practical, and so on. Designed to help the ordinary person without seminary training to use these approaches.

Fee, Gordon, and Douglas Stuart. *How to Read the Bible For All Its Worth* (Zondervan, 1982).
After explaining in general what interpretation (exegesis) and application (hermeneutics) are, Fee and Stuart offer chapters on interpreting and applying the different kinds of writing in the Bible: Epistles, Gospels, Old Testament Law, Old Testament narrative, the Prophets, Psalms, Wisdom, and Revelation. Fee and Stuart also suggest good commentaries on each biblical book. They write as evangelical scholars who personally recognize Scripture as God's Word for their daily lives.

Jensen, Irving L. *Independent Bible Study* (Moody, 1963), and *Enjoy Your Bible* (Moody, 1962).

The former is a comprehensive introduction to the inductive Bible study method, especially the use of synthetic charts. The latter is a simpler introduction to the subject.

Wald, Oletta. *The Joy of Discovery in Bible Study* (Augsburg, 1975).

Wald focuses on issues such as how to observe all that is in a text, how to ask questions of a text, how to use grammar and passage structure to see the writer's point, and so on. Very helpful on these subjects.

Other titles in the *Lifechange* series you may be interested in: